9

FORMULAS

FOR

FINANCIAL FREEDOM

Mastering Money Management
and
Wealth Building

M. D. Lloyd (PhD)

DEDICATION

To all those who dare to dream, strive to achieve, and orchestrate their own symphony of financial freedom.

Your unwavering dedication and commitment inspire us to compose a life of abundance, empowerment, and impact.

May this book serve as a guiding melody on your journey toward mastering money management and building lasting wealth.

M. D. Lloyd (PhD)

CONTENTS

ACKNOWLEDGMENTS

I would like to express my heartfelt gratitude to all those who contributed to the creation of this book, **"9 Formulas for Financial Freedom: Mastering Money Management and Wealth Building."** This endeavor would not have been possible without the collective efforts and support of many individuals.

I am deeply appreciative of the invaluable insights and wisdom shared by mentors, colleagues, and experts in the fields of finance, wealth management, and personal development. Your guidance has shaped the content of this book and enriched its message.

I extend my thanks to my family and friends, whose unwavering encouragement and belief in my vision fueled my determination to bring this book to fruition. Your support has been a constant source of inspiration.

I am grateful for the diligent work of the editorial and publishing teams, whose expertise and dedication transformed the manuscript into a polished work. Your commitment to excellence has ensured the quality of this book.

Lastly, I express my profound appreciation to the readers, individuals seeking to enhance their financial literacy and embark on a journey to financial freedom. It is my sincere hope that the insights and formulas presented within these pages will serve as a compass guiding you toward prosperity and fulfillment.

With utmost respect and gratitude,
M. D. Lloyd (PhD)

INTRODUCTION

In the quiet corners of my memory, there's a scene that remains vivid a scene that encapsulates the essence of my journey from financial struggle to success. I find myself transported back to a small, dimly lit room, its walls echoing with the hum of frustration and the weight of uncertainty. There, seated at the worn kitchen table, surrounded by stacks of unpaid bills and looming financial obligations, I felt a sense of helplessness that seemed insurmountable.

This wasn't the life I had imagined for myself. Growing up, I had been instilled with dreams of grandeur, told that with hard work, success was inevitable. But as I stared at those unpaid bills, it became painfully clear that hard work alone wasn't enough. The missing piece of the puzzle, the secret that had eluded me for so long, was financial education a topic rarely taught in schools but one that holds the key to unlocking the doors of prosperity.

My journey began that day, a fervent quest for knowledge that led me down a path of self-discovery, empowerment, and ultimately, financial freedom. It was a journey that highlighted a fundamental truth: that true wealth is not merely about the size of your bank account, but about the knowledge and mindset you possess.

It was during this transformative period that I stumbled upon the concept that would become the cornerstone of my financial philosophy the 9 Formulas for Financial Freedom. These formulas, each representing a crucial aspect of money management and wealth building, are the result of years of learning, experimenting, and adapting. They are the distilled wisdom that emerged from the pages of countless books, the lessons I gleaned from mentors and advisors, and the insights I gained through both triumphs and failures.

Now, as I stand on the other side of that once-imposing financial struggle, I am compelled to share these formulas with you. I believe, wholeheartedly, that financial freedom is within your grasp, no matter where you are starting from. Just as I discovered the transformational power of financial education and mindset, I am committed to guiding you toward the same realization.

In the pages that follow, we will embark on a journey together a journey that transcends mere numbers and balance sheets. It is a journey that delves into the very core of our beliefs, attitudes, and habits surrounding money. It is a journey that will empower you to take control of your financial destiny, to rewrite the narrative of your life, and to chart a course toward the true freedom that comes from mastering money management and wealth building.

The 9 Formulas for Financial Freedom are not a quick fix or a magic formula for instant riches. They are, however, a roadmap a blueprint that, when followed with dedication and intention, can pave the way to a life of abundance, purpose, and fulfillment. As you immerse yourself in the pages ahead, I encourage you to keep an open mind, to challenge your preconceived notions, and to be willing to embrace change.

Remember, financial education is not a destination; it is a lifelong journey. And just as every step you take brings you closer to your goals, every nugget of wisdom you absorb brings you closer to the financial freedom you deserve. So, let's begin this journey together. Let's dive into the 9 Formulas for Financial Freedom and uncover the tools that will empower you to master money management, build lasting wealth, and claim the life of your dreams.

THE FOUNDATION FORMULA
Mind Your Mindset

In the pursuit of financial freedom, the path to success begins not with complex strategies or advanced investment techniques, but with something far more powerful and fundamental: your mindset. Your thoughts, beliefs, and attitudes towards money shape the actions you take and the outcomes you achieve. Welcome to the cornerstone of wealth-building excellence – The Foundation Formula: Mind Your Mindset.

Unveiling the Mindset-Money Connection

Imagine your mindset as the compass guiding your financial journey. Just as a ship's course is set by the orientation of its compass, your financial trajectory is determined by your mindset. This fundamental principle underscores the symbiotic relationship between your thoughts and your financial reality.

The mindset-money connection is rooted in the psychological phenomenon known as the "self-fulfilling prophecy." If you believe you are destined to struggle financially, your actions will unconsciously align with that belief, reinforcing the struggle. Conversely, if you hold the conviction that you are capable of achieving financial abundance, your actions will reflect this confidence, propelling you towards prosperity.

Cultivating a Wealth-Worthy Mindset

Shifting from a scarcity mindset to a wealth-worthy mindset requires intentional effort and self-awareness. Here are key principles to foster a mindset primed for financial success:

1. Embrace Abundance

Recognize that the universe is abundant, and there is an abundance of opportunities, resources, and wealth available. Reject notions of scarcity that breed fear and hesitation. Embrace a mindset of abundance to open yourself to new possibilities.

2. Transform Fear into Opportunity

See difficulties and failures as learning opportunities rather than as insurmountable hurdles. Fear often paralyzes progress; a wealth-worthy mindset thrives on using fear as fuel for forward momentum.

3. Empower Yourself with Knowledge

Learn about investing, wealth-building methods, and personal finance. Knowledge empowers you to make informed decisions, reducing anxiety and enhancing your ability to seize opportunities.

4. Practice Gratitude

Have an attitude of gratitude for your possessions and achievements. Gratitude shifts your focus from what is lacking to the abundance present in your life, attracting more positive experiences.

5. Visualize Success

Envision your financial goals with vivid clarity. Regularly visualize yourself living the life you desire, feeling the emotions associated with achieving those goals. Visualization creates a powerful mental blueprint that guides your actions.

6. Embrace Continuous Learning

A wealth-worthy mindset thrives on continuous learning and adaptation. Stay curious and open to new ideas, strategies, and perspectives that can enhance your financial acumen.

7. Surround Yourself with Positivity

Surround yourself with individuals who uplift and support your financial aspirations. The company you keep greatly influences your mindset and, consequently, your financial success.

The Role of Mindset in Shaping Financial Outcomes

Delving into the intricate interplay between mindset and financial outcomes reveals a profound connection that transcends mere coincidence. The role of mindset in shaping one's financial destiny is akin to the sculptor's chisel shaping a block of marble it carves the contours, defines the edges, and determines the final masterpiece.

In this intricate dance between thoughts and financial realities, mindset emerges as the silent architect. It wields the power to influence decisions, inspire actions, and steer the course of financial endeavors. Like a rudder guiding a ship through turbulent waters, mindset navigates individuals through the uncertain seas of economic landscapes.

The mindset you adopt acts as a lens through which you perceive opportunities and challenges. A scarcity mindset may cast a shadow over potential gains, focusing disproportionately on perceived risks and limitations. On the other hand, a mindset of abundance illuminates the path, spotlighting opportunities that might otherwise remain hidden.

Consider, for instance, how a growth-oriented mindset can propel individuals to embrace calculated risks, driving them to explore innovative investment avenues. This mindset is anchored in the belief that setbacks are stepping stones, and adversity is a catalyst for adaptation and growth. Such mental frameworks foster resilience, enabling individuals to weather financial storms and emerge stronger, equipped with valuable lessons.

Conversely, a fixed mindset, resistant to change and growth, might hinder one's ability to seize emerging opportunities. The fear of failure, deeply embedded in this mindset, could deter individuals from pursuing ventures that could potentially yield substantial financial gains.

Mindset's role in shaping financial outcomes extends beyond isolated decisions. It weaves into the fabric of long-term wealth-building strategies. A forward-thinking mindset encourages strategic planning, prompting individuals to invest in education, acquire new skills, and diversify their financial portfolios. This mindset is rooted in the understanding that wealth is not just accumulated but cultivated through conscious, well-informed choices.

In contrast, a short-term, instant gratification mindset may lead to impulsive financial decisions, disregarding the importance of delayed gratification and disciplined savings. The long-term consequences of such a mindset could include missed opportunities for compounding growth and financial security.

In the realm of entrepreneurship and business, mindset becomes even more pivotal. Visionaries who envision and manifest transformative ventures often share a common thread – an unwavering belief in their capacity to create impact and generate wealth. This entrepreneurial mindset propels them to take calculated risks, persevere through setbacks, and persistently innovate, ultimately reshaping industries and redefining financial landscapes.

In conclusion, the role of mindset in shaping financial outcomes is undeniably potent. It is the silent force that shapes decisions, steers actions, and ultimately sculpts the financial trajectory of individuals and enterprises. By recognizing and harnessing this influence, individuals can empower themselves to consciously cultivate a mindset that aligns with their financial aspirations, fostering a future of abundance, resilience, and well-earned success.

The Difference Between an Abundance Mindset and a Scarcity Mindset

At the core of an individual's perception and approach to life lies a fundamental duality: the scarcity mindset and the abundance mindset. These contrasting mindsets form the lenses through which we interpret the world around us and, in turn, shape our behaviors, decisions, and overall experiences.

The scarcity mindset is characterized by a lens that magnifies limitations, constraints, and perceived deficiencies. Those who operate from this mindset tend to fixate on what is lacking, be it material resources, opportunities, time, or even personal qualities. Every setback is amplified, every challenge appears insurmountable, and fear often becomes the driving force behind decision-making.

From a financial perspective, a scarcity mindset can manifest as a paralyzing fear of financial loss, leading to reluctance in taking calculated risks or seizing investment opportunities. The focus on scarcity might lead to a relentless pursuit of immediate gains, disregarding the potential for long-term wealth growth. This mindset can also breed unhealthy competition and comparison, as individuals feel compelled to guard and hoard what little they have rather than collaborate or share.

On the other end of the spectrum lies the abundance mindset a perspective rooted in the belief that possibilities are vast, opportunities are abundant, and resources are plentiful. Individuals with an abundance mindset are more inclined to see setbacks as temporary and challenges as stepping stones to growth. They possess a deep-seated confidence in their ability to adapt, learn, and create, regardless of the circumstances.

In the context of personal finance, an abundance mindset encourages individuals to approach money with a sense of gratitude and responsibility. Instead of dwelling on what they lack, they focus on what they have and how they can leverage it to generate more value. This mindset fosters a willingness to invest in self-improvement, education, and strategic financial planning. An abundance mindset also promotes collaboration and generosity, as those who hold it are more likely to share knowledge, resources, and opportunities, believing that there is enough for everyone.

The scarcity mindset often leads to a cycle of limitation and stagnation, reinforcing negative beliefs and inhibiting growth. Conversely, the abundance mindset acts as a catalyst for expansion, innovation, and progress. It emboldens individuals to pursue their passions, take calculated risks, and embrace change, ultimately leading to a life that is more fulfilling, purpose-driven, and financially rewarding.

In essence, the difference between a scarcity mindset and an abundance mindset lies in their perspectives on limitation and possibility. While the scarcity mindset constrains potential, the abundance mindset fuels it. By cultivating an awareness of these mindsets and actively nurturing an abundance-oriented perspective, individuals can unlock a world of opportunities, create lasting wealth, and embark on a journey towards greater financial freedom and overall well-being.

QUOTE:

Scarcity Mindset:

"A scarcity mindset chains you to self-imposed constraints and bars your potential. Break free, for the universe offers boundless opportunities waiting to be embraced."

Abundance Mindset:

"Embrace the abundance mindset, and watch your world transform. Where scarcity breeds fear, abundance ignites courage, propelling you to create, share, and thrive."

Scarcity vs. Abundance:

"In the realm of possibility, two mindsets clash. Scarcity whispers defeat, while abundance roars triumph. Choose wisely, for your mindset shapes the destiny you manifest."

Practical Strategies to Cultivate a Wealth-Oriented Mindset

Cultivating a mindset that aligns with wealth

creation requires a deliberate and persistent effort. The journey from a scarcity-oriented mentality to a wealth-oriented mindset is transformative, empowering you to navigate the complex world of finances with confidence and purpose. Here, we unveil practical strategies that serve as stepping stones on this path of mindset evolution:

Practice Gratitude Daily: Begin and end each day by acknowledging the abundance already present in your life. Gratitude shifts your focus from what you lack to what you possess, fostering a positive perspective that attracts further prosperity.

Visualize Your Success: Envision your financial goals as vividly as possible. Close your eyes and feel the emotions associated with achieving those goals. Visualization creates a mental blueprint that guides your actions and decisions.

Challenge Negative Beliefs: Identify and challenge any limiting beliefs you hold about money and wealth. Replace them with empowering affirmations that reinforce your capabilities and worthiness of success.

Seek Learning Opportunities: Commit to lifelong learning in the realm of finance. Educate yourself about investment strategies, personal finance, and money management. Knowledge dispels fear and empowers you to make informed decisions.

Surround Yourself with Abundance: Surround yourself with individuals who exemplify a wealth-oriented mindset. Engage in conversations that inspire, share ideas, and create an environment conducive to growth.

Embrace Risks as Opportunities: Shift your perspective on risk-taking. View calculated risks as stepping stones toward growth rather than as potential pitfalls. Each risk you take is an opportunity for valuable experience and learning.

Set Purpose-Driven Goals: Align your financial goals with your deeper purpose and values. Connecting wealth-building to a greater purpose fuels your motivation and enhances the meaning behind your actions.

Concentrate on Finding Solutions, Not Problems: When faced with difficulties, focus your efforts on doing so rather than wallowing in difficulties. A wealth-oriented mindset thrives on problem-solving and resourcefulness.

Practice Generosity: Cultivate a spirit of giving and sharing. Generosity fosters a sense of abundance and attracts positive energy, which can lead to unexpected opportunities.

Celebrate Small Wins: Acknowledge and celebrate your financial achievements, no matter how modest they may seem. Each step forward reinforces the belief that you are making progress toward your ultimate goals.

Remember, cultivating a wealth-oriented mindset is a journey, not an overnight transformation. It requires consistent effort, self-awareness, and a commitment to growth. As you integrate these strategies into your daily life, you'll find yourself stepping into a world where possibilities are endless and your potential for financial success knows no bounds.

QUOTE:

"The blueprint for your financial future is inside your thoughts. Choose the brush of abundance, the palette of perseverance, and paint a masterpiece of prosperity that leaves an indelible mark on the canvas of your life."

How a Positive Mindset Can Lead to Better Financial Decisions and Opportunities?

A positive mindset serves as a powerful catalyst that

not only shapes our perceptions of the world but also influences the financial decisions we make and the opportunities we attract. When we view our financial landscape through the lens of positivity, we unlock a realm of possibilities that might otherwise remain concealed by doubt or fear. Let's explore how cultivating a positive mindset can lead to enhanced financial decisions and a horizon of abundant opportunities:

Clarity Amidst Complexity: A positive mindset sharpens our ability to make clear and rational financial decisions. When we approach challenges with optimism, we are more likely to assess situations objectively, weigh pros and cons, and arrive at well-informed choices that align with our long-term goals.

Risk as a Stepping Stone: Embracing a positive outlook empowers us to perceive risks not as obstacles, but as stepping stones to growth. By focusing on the potential rewards rather than fixating on potential losses, we become more open to calculated risks that can propel us toward lucrative opportunities.

Adaptability and Innovation: Positivity nurtures our capacity to adapt and innovate. In the face of financial setbacks, a positive mindset encourages us to seek creative solutions and explore alternative paths. This resilience enables us to weather storms and pivot toward unforeseen opportunities.

Confidence Breeds Confidence: A positive mindset breeds self-confidence, a trait that resonates with potential investors, partners, and collaborators. When we exude confidence in our financial pursuits, we attract like-minded individuals who are drawn to our vision, amplifying our opportunities for growth and success.

Networking and Collaboration: A positive outlook fuels a willingness to connect and collaborate. Building a robust network opens doors to joint ventures, mentorship, and partnerships that can exponentially expand our financial horizons.

Magnetism for Abundance: Positivity acts as a magnetic force that attracts abundance. When we radiate positivity, we generate an aura of possibility and opportunity. This aura becomes a beacon, drawing favorable circumstances and influential individuals into our financial sphere.

Responsible Financial Management: A positive mindset fosters a sense of responsibility and stewardship over our financial resources. With an optimistic perspective, we are more likely to allocate our funds wisely, save diligently, and make investments that align with our aspirations.

In conclusion, a positive mindset is more than just a state of mind it's a gateway to a world of improved financial decision-making and expanded opportunities. By embracing positivity, we illuminate the path toward prosperity, foster resilience in the face of challenges, and open ourselves to a spectrum of possibilities previously unimagined.

QUOTE:

Each optimistic thinking we have is a thread of opportunity in the tapestry of finance. As we craft our mindset with optimism, we cast a net that captures the boundless wealth of the universe."

Conclusion: Your Mindset, Your Wealth

As we embark on this transformative journey through the Foundation Formula of mindset mastery, remember that the true essence of financial freedom begins within you. The beliefs you hold, the thoughts you nurture, and the actions you take are the bedrock upon which your financial future is built.

In the chapters ahead, we will delve deeper into the other eight formulas that, when combined with a wealth-worthy mindset, will empower you to achieve unparalleled financial freedom. The path may not always be easy, but with the right mindset, you possess the resilience, determination, and ingenuity to overcome any challenge and create the life of abundance you deserve.

Get ready to unlock the doors to financial freedom as we explore the transformative power of the nine formulas for mastering money management and wealth building. Your journey begins here, with the Foundation Formula – Mind Your Mindset.

THE WEALTH BLUEPRINT FORMULA
Design Your Financial Plan

In the grand symphony of financial success, every masterpiece begins with a meticulously crafted blueprint. Just as an architect sketches the foundations of a towering structure, you, too, hold the power to design the blueprint for your financial future. Welcome to The Second Formula of "9 Formulas for Financial Freedom: Mastering Money Management and Wealth Building" – The Wealth Blueprint Formula.

The Art of Financial Design

Consider your financial blueprint as a map that guides you through uncharted terrain. This blueprint doesn't just chart your course; it lays the groundwork for your financial aspirations, ensuring they transform from dreams into reality. The Wealth Blueprint Formula is the compass that directs you toward financial abundance and freedom.

At its core, The Wealth Blueprint Formula is a strategic framework that encompasses your financial goals, aspirations, income streams, investments, and savings. It is a roadmap that harmonizes your resources with your dreams, ensuring that every financial decision is a deliberate step toward your desired destination.

Crafting Your Wealth Blueprint

Step 1: Define Your Goals

Begin by setting clear, specific, and measurable financial goals. Whether it's achieving a certain level of passive income, purchasing a home, or funding your dream venture, your goals shape the foundation of your blueprint.

Step 2: Assess Your Current Situation

Conduct a comprehensive assessment of your

current financial state. Understand your income, expenses, debts, and assets. This assessment acts as a starting point, allowing you to gauge your progress as you move forward.

Step 3: Create a Budget

Craft a detailed budget that allocates your income toward essential expenses, savings, investments, and discretionary spending. A well-structured budget ensures that your financial decisions are aligned with your long-term goals.

Step 4: Diversify Income Streams

Explore diverse avenues for generating income. Whether through a primary job, side hustles, investments, or passive income sources, diversification safeguards your financial stability and accelerates your journey to wealth.

Step 5: Invest Wisely

Develop a strategic investment plan that aligns with

your risk tolerance and goals. Invest in assets that have the potential to grow over time, such as stocks, real estate, or mutual funds.

Step 6: Plan for Retirement

Incorporate a solid retirement plan into your blueprint. Consider setting up retirement accounts, such as a 401(k) or an IRA, to ensure a secure financial future during your golden years.

Step 7: Emergency Fund and Insurance

Build an emergency fund to safeguard against unexpected financial setbacks. Additionally, evaluate and secure appropriate insurance coverage to protect your assets and loved ones.

Step 8: Review and Adjust

Regularly review your wealth blueprint to track progress and make necessary adjustments. Life evolves, and your financial plan should evolve with it to remain effective and relevant.

The Significance of Creating a Clear Financial Blueprint

Crafting a clear financial blueprint is akin to embarking on a purposeful journey armed with a detailed map. It serves as a guiding light that illuminates your path through the intricate landscape of money management and wealth building. The significance of creating such a blueprint lies in its ability to transform your financial aspirations from abstract notions into well-defined, achievable goals. Here's why a clear financial blueprint is of paramount importance:

Direction Amidst Chaos: Life's financial terrain is rife with uncertainty and complexity. A well-structured financial blueprint acts as a compass, providing clear direction amidst the chaos. It empowers you to make informed decisions, ensuring that every financial step you take is aligned with your ultimate objectives.

Goal Clarity: A financial blueprint lends clarity to your goals. By articulating your aspirations in tangible terms, you create a concrete roadmap that outlines the specific achievements you aim to attain. This clarity fuels your motivation and enhances your focus, driving you to strive for consistent progress.

Resource Allocation: One of the most significant advantages of a financial blueprint is its ability to allocate your resources optimally. With a detailed plan in place, you can allocate your income strategically, channeling funds towards essential expenses, savings, investments, and discretionary spending in a balanced manner.

Empowered Decision-Making: Decisions regarding money can be daunting, especially in the absence of a guiding framework. A well-crafted financial blueprint equips you with the confidence to make empowered decisions. It provides you with a reference point against which you can evaluate the potential outcomes of each choice.

Long-Term Vision: Your financial blueprint isn't limited to immediate gains; it extends into the future. By incorporating long-term financial goals, such as retirement planning and wealth preservation, your blueprint encourages you to think beyond the present moment, fostering a legacy that endures for generations to come.

Adaptability and Flexibility: While a blueprint provides structure, it also acknowledges the need for adaptability. Life is marked by unexpected twists and turns, and a well-designed financial blueprint takes these into account. It allows for adjustments and refinements as circumstances evolve, ensuring your financial plan remains relevant.

Financial Discipline: Creating a financial blueprint cultivates a sense of discipline. It encourages you to adhere to your budget, resist impulsive spending, and stay committed to your goals. This discipline is key to maintaining financial stability and progress over time.

Reduced Stress: Financial uncertainty can lead to stress and anxiety. A clear financial blueprint alleviates this stress by offering a sense of control and predictability. It provides a structured framework that eases worry and fosters a more harmonious relationship with your finances.

In essence, a clear financial blueprint is the cornerstone of your financial success. It transcends being a mere document; it is a dynamic tool that empowers you to navigate the vast sea of financial choices with clarity, purpose, and resilience. By creating and adhering to your financial blueprint, you embark on a journey of empowerment, fulfillment, and ultimately, the realization of your dreams.

QUOTE:

"Like an architect sketches a vision into reality, a clear financial blueprint transforms dreams into attainable goals. With every detail etched, you forge a path to prosperity that only your unwavering commitment can pave."

The Process of Setting Financial Goals and Creating a Plan to Achieve Them

Navigating the terrain of financial success begins with a deliberate and strategic approach to goal setting and planning. This transformative process empowers you to shape your financial destiny with intention and purpose. Here's a step-by-step guide to assist you in setting meaningful financial goals and crafting a comprehensive plan to achieve them:

Step 1: Self-Reflection and Vision Building

Begin by engaging in a deep introspection of your values, aspirations, and long-term vision. Consider the life you envision for yourself, your family, and your future. Define your overarching financial objectives that align with this vision.

Step 2: Set Specific Goals

Break down your overarching objectives into specific, measurable, achievable, relevant, and time-bound (SMART) goals. Whether it's buying a home, paying off debt, building an emergency fund, or funding your children's education, articulate each goal with precision.

Step 3: Prioritize Goals

Determine the order of importance for your goals. Assign priority based on their significance and your current financial situation. This ensures that your focus remains aligned with your immediate and long-term aspirations.

Step 4: Quantify Your Goals

Attach a monetary value and timeline to each goal.

Specify the amount you need to achieve, the timeframe within which you aim to accomplish it, and any milestones along the way.

Step 5: Assess Your Current Financial Situation

Conduct a comprehensive assessment of your current financial state. Evaluate your income, expenses, debts, assets, and existing investments. This evaluation serves as the foundation upon which you'll build your financial plan.

Step 6: Develop a Budget

Craft a detailed budget that allocates your income to your various goals, essential expenses, savings, investments, and discretionary spending. Your budget acts as a strategic tool that guides your financial decisions on a day-to-day basis.

Step 7: Explore Income Streams

Diversify your income streams to enhance your financial stability and accelerate goal achievement.

Consider additional sources of income, such as side gigs, freelancing, or investments, to bolster your financial resources.

Step 8: Create an Action Plan

Break down each goal into actionable steps. Determine the specific actions, milestones, and deadlines required to progress toward achieving your goals. Your action plan serves as a roadmap that keeps you on track.

Step 9: Monitor and Adjust

Regularly review your progress against your financial goals. Make necessary adjustments to your plan as circumstances change or new opportunities arise. Flexibility is key to ensuring your plan remains relevant and effective.

Step 10: Celebrate Achievements

Acknowledge and celebrate your achievements along the way. Your effort and dedication are demonstrated by each milestone you achieve. Celebrating successes fuels your motivation and reinforces your determination to persevere.

In embracing this comprehensive approach to goal setting and financial planning, you embark on a journey of empowerment and transformation. By aligning your financial decisions with your aspirations and implementing a well-structured plan, you carve a path that leads to the fulfillment of your dreams.

"Within the blueprint of your dreams lies the design for your financial reality. As you set goals and craft your plan, remember that every intention is a brushstroke, and every action a stroke of genius."

The Importance of Diversification and Risk Management in a Wealth-Building Strategy

In the intricate tapestry of wealth-building, two crucial threads intricately interweave: diversification and risk management. These twin pillars form the foundation upon which a robust and sustainable financial future is constructed. Let us delve into the profound importance of these principles in sculpting a successful wealth-building strategy:

Diversification: Safeguarding Your Prosperity

Diversification embodies the principle of not putting all your eggs in one basket. It's the strategic act of spreading investments across a variety of asset classes, industries, and geographic regions. This strategic distribution serves as a financial safety net, shielding you from the volatility inherent in any single market or sector.

Risk Mitigation: Diversification is your shield against market turbulence. By allocating your resources across diverse assets, you mitigate the impact of a poor-performing investment. When one asset falters, the strength of others cushions the blow, reducing the overall risk to your portfolio.

Capital Preservation: Preserving your capital is paramount in wealth-building. Diversification minimizes the potential for catastrophic losses, allowing you to retain a greater portion of your investment capital even during challenging economic periods.

Optimized Returns: Different assets perform well under varying market conditions. Diversification optimizes returns by capturing gains from sectors experiencing growth while offsetting losses from those undergoing contraction.

Liquidity and Flexibility: A diversified portfolio enhances your liquidity and flexibility. In times of need, you can liquidate certain assets without being solely dependent on the performance of a single investment.

Risk Management: Navigating Financial Waters

Risk management is the compass that guides your journey toward wealth. It entails identifying potential risks, analyzing their potential impact, and implementing strategies to mitigate or avoid them. Effective risk management ensures that your wealth-building strategy remains resilient in the face of adversity.

Preservation of Capital: Mitigating risk preserves your hard-earned capital. Through careful evaluation and precautionary measures, you shield your investments from unnecessary exposure to unforeseen challenges.

Long-Term Sustainability: A sound risk management strategy promotes long-term sustainability. By anticipating and planning for potential pitfalls, you enhance your capacity to weather economic downturns and emerge stronger on the other side.

Confidence in Decision-Making: A well-structured risk management plan empowers you to make informed decisions. It eliminates impulsive actions driven by fear or market volatility, fostering a sense of confidence in your investment choices.

Steady Progress: Consistent risk management encourages steady progress toward your financial goals. Instead of being derailed by unexpected setbacks, you adapt and adjust, maintaining a steady trajectory toward wealth accumulation.

In the symphony of wealth-building, diversification and risk management harmonize to create a melody of stability, growth, and prosperity. By integrating these principles into your financial strategy, you lay the groundwork for a resilient and enduring path toward the realization of your financial dreams.

QUOTE:

"In the realm of wealth-building, diversification is the palette of possibility, and risk management is the brush of prudence. Together, they paint a masterpiece of financial resilience that stands strong against the winds of uncertainty."

Examples of Successful Individuals Who Crafted Effective Wealth Blueprints

The annals of financial history are rich with stories of individuals who, armed with strategic vision and unwavering determination, crafted remarkable wealth blueprints that transformed their aspirations into reality. These success stories serve as beacons of inspiration, demonstrating the power of intentional planning and disciplined execution. Here are a few notable examples:

Warren Buffett - The Oracle of Omaha: Often hailed as one of the greatest investors of all time,

Warren Buffett's wealth blueprint is founded on the principles of value investing and prudent decision-making. His steadfast adherence to a long-term investment approach, coupled with the strategic acquisition of undervalued assets, propelled him to build an empire through his company, Berkshire Hathaway.

Oprah Winfrey - Media Mogul and Philanthropist: Oprah Winfrey's wealth blueprint is a testament to the intersection of passion and purpose. From her humble beginnings, she strategically leveraged her unique strengths in media and communication to create a multimedia empire. By connecting with her audience authentically and diversifying her ventures, Oprah's wealth blueprint exemplifies the synergy of entrepreneurship and personal brand development.

Elon Musk - Visionary Entrepreneur: Elon Musk's wealth blueprint embodies audacious goals and calculated risk-taking. Through his ventures such as Tesla, SpaceX, and SolarCity, Musk has revolutionized industries and amassed significant wealth. His visionary approach, knack for innovation, and willingness to tackle seemingly insurmountable challenges are central to his wealth-building journey.

Sara Blakely - Founder of Spanx: Sara Blakely's wealth blueprint is a tale of turning adversity into opportunity. As the founder of Spanx, she identified a gap in the market and pioneered a new product category. Her story underscores the significance of creativity, perseverance, and the ability to identify untapped niches.

Robert Kiyosaki - Author and Entrepreneur: Robert Kiyosaki's wealth blueprint is rooted in financial education and real estate investing. Through his "Rich Dad Poor Dad" series, Kiyosaki emphasized the importance of financial literacy and passive income streams. His blueprint encourages individuals to think beyond traditional employment and take control of their financial destinies.

Mark Zuckerberg - Co-Founder of Facebook:
Mark Zuckerberg's wealth blueprint exemplifies the transformative potential of technological innovation. His creation of Facebook, fueled by a clear vision of connecting people globally, evolved into a social media giant. Zuckerberg's blueprint underscores the power of identifying societal needs and leveraging technology to fulfill them.

These individuals, among others, showcase that effective wealth blueprints are diverse in nature, reflecting unique strengths, passions, and market insights. While their paths differ, the common thread lies in their ability to strategically align their aspirations with deliberate actions, adapt to challenges, and persevere toward their goals. Their stories stand as reminders that with vision, planning, and determination, anyone can craft a blueprint that paves the way to financial success and enduring legacy.

Conclusion: Blueprint Your Destiny

As you embark on the journey of crafting your wealth blueprint, remember that every stroke of the pen holds the potential to shape your financial destiny. The Wealth Blueprint Formula empowers you to architect a life of abundance, guiding you through financial decisions with purpose and intention.

In the upcoming chapters, we will delve deeper into the remaining formulas that, when interwoven with your wealth blueprint, will pave the way to unparalleled financial freedom. Remember, you are the master designer, and every stroke of intention brings you closer to the masterpiece of financial success you deserve.

QUOTE:

"Your wealth blueprint is the masterpiece you create, a testament to your dreams and determination. With each stroke of strategic design, you paint a brighter future, a canvas alive with the colors of prosperity."

THE INCOME ACCELERATOR FORMULA
Multiply Your Earnings

In the symphony of financial growth, the quest to amass wealth is harmoniously orchestrated by the rhythm of earnings. Welcome to the Third Formula of "9 Formulas for Financial Freedom: Mastering Money Management and Wealth Building" – The Income Accelerator Formula. Within these pages, we uncover the transformative art of expanding your income streams and propelling your earning potential to new heights.

Unleashing the Power of Multiplicity

Imagine your income as a garden of possibilities, with each stream a vibrant blossom. The Income Accelerator Formula is your cultivator, nurturing and expanding these blossoms to create a lush landscape of financial abundance. This formula transcends traditional employment, inviting you to harness various avenues to amplify your earnings.

The essence of The Income Accelerator Formula lies in its ability to magnify your financial inflow through a strategic blend of innovation, diversification, and value creation.

The Path to Earning Multiplicity

Step 1: Identify Your Strengths and Passions

Discover your unique talents, skills, and passions. By aligning your income-generating endeavors with what you excel at and love, you set the stage for sustainable and fulfilling earning potential.

Step 2: Explore Diverse Income Streams

Expand beyond the confines of a single paycheck. Seek opportunities for additional income streams such as freelancing, consulting, investing, royalties, e-commerce, and real estate. Diversification enhances your financial stability and accelerates wealth accumulation.

Step 3: Innovate and Create Value

Innovation is the catalyst that propels your income to new heights. Identify gaps in the market, offer innovative solutions, and consistently deliver value to your clients or customers. The ability to solve problems and meet needs sets you on the path to becoming an income accelerator.

Step 4: Leverage Technology and Automation

Embrace technology to amplify your reach and efficiency. Leverage automation tools, online platforms, and e-commerce to scale your income streams while minimizing time constraints.

Step 5: Network and Collaborate

Forge meaningful connections within your industry and beyond. Networking opens doors to joint ventures, partnerships, and collaborations that can exponentially expand your earning opportunities.

Step 6: Continual Learning and Growth

Commit to continuous learning and skill development. As you enhance your expertise, you position yourself as a valuable asset, enabling you to command higher rates and seize emerging income opportunities.

Step 7: Monitor and Optimize

Regularly assess the performance of your income streams. Identify which streams are flourishing and which need refinement. Optimization ensures that your efforts yield maximum financial returns.

The Value of Increasing One's Earning Potential

In the realm of financial empowerment, the value of increasing one's earning potential is a beacon that illuminates the path to a life of greater opportunity, security, and fulfillment. This pursuit transcends the mere accumulation of wealth; it represents a profound investment in oneself that yields multifaceted rewards. Let us explore the significance of expanding your earning potential and the transformative impact it can have on your journey to financial freedom:

Opening Doors of Opportunity: Increasing your earning potential widens the spectrum of opportunities that come within your reach. With enhanced income capabilities, you are equipped to pursue ventures, experiences, and aspirations that were once beyond your grasp. These newfound opportunities act as stepping stones toward realizing your dreams.

Empowerment and Autonomy: A higher earning potential grants you a greater degree of autonomy over your life. It frees you from the constraints of financial limitations, empowering you to make choices based on passion, purpose, and personal fulfillment rather than necessity.

Financial Security and Resilience: An elevated

earning potential provides a safety net that cushions against unexpected setbacks and economic downturns. Financial security becomes a cornerstone, allowing you to navigate challenges with resilience and confidence, knowing that you have the resources to weather storms.

Investment in Self-Growth: The journey to increase your earning potential often necessitates continuous learning, skill development, and self-improvement. This investment in personal growth not only enhances your capabilities but also enriches your life with new knowledge, experiences, and perspectives.

Legacy and Generational Impact: Elevating your earning potential extends its benefits to future generations. By setting an example of dedication, ambition, and hard work, you inspire others to strive for their own financial empowerment. The legacy of your efforts can shape the trajectory of your family's financial well-being.

Contributing to Society: As your earning potential expands, so does your capacity to give back to your community and causes you believe in. Your financial resources become a tool for positive impact, enabling you to support charitable endeavors, philanthropic initiatives, and social change.

Personal Fulfillment: Achieving higher earning potential often aligns with pursuing work that resonates with your passions and values. The fulfillment derived from engaging in meaningful, purpose-driven endeavors enriches your overall well-being and quality of life.

Unleashing Creativity and Innovation: With a heightened earning potential, you're afforded the freedom to explore innovative ideas and entrepreneurial pursuits. This unleashes your creativity, encourages out-of-the-box thinking, and fosters a culture of innovation.

In the grand tapestry of financial growth, increasing your earning potential emerges as a cornerstone, a pivotal force that unlocks the doors to a life imbued with possibility and prosperity. It embodies the spirit of continuous improvement, personal empowerment, and the unwavering belief that your potential knows no bounds.

QUOTE:

"You have the ability to increase your earning potential; there are a wealth of unrealized opportunities just waiting to be discovered. As you embark on this journey, remember that your efforts not only shape your financial future but also weave threads of inspiration for others to follow."

An Insights into Leveraging Skills, Education, And Networking to Boost Income

Harnessing the triumvirate of skills, education, and networking is a transformative strategy that propels you toward an elevated income trajectory. These pillars serve as catalysts, each reinforcing the other, creating a synergy that amplifies your earning potential. Let's delve into the insights that unveil the art of leveraging these forces to boost your income:

1. Skills: The Currency of Value

Skills are the cornerstone of your professional currency, and their mastery directly influences your marketability and earning capacity. Cultivate a mindset of continuous improvement and skill development, for it is the acquisition and honing of these talents that sets you apart in a competitive landscape.

Identify and Develop: Identify the skills that are relevant to your industry and align with your career aspirations. Invest time and effort in developing these skills through formal education, online courses, workshops, and hands-on experience.

Specialization and Expertise: Become an expert in a niche area that is in demand. Specialization enhances your perceived value and enables you to command premium rates for your services.

Adaptability: Stay attuned to industry trends and technological advancements. Adapt your skill set to meet evolving demands, ensuring that you remain relevant in a dynamic marketplace.

2. Education: Igniting Knowledge and Growth

Education is the cornerstone of empowerment, and its impact extends beyond formal degrees. It encompasses a lifelong pursuit of learning, self-discovery, and intellectual growth that enriches your perspective and enhances your earning potential.

Formal and Informal Learning: While degrees have their merits, recognize that informal learning is equally valuable. Engage in self-study, read voraciously, attend seminars, and participate in online courses to broaden your horizons.

Skill-Enhancing Education: Seek education that directly enhances your skills and expertise. Acquiring certifications or taking courses that align with your career goals can significantly boost your credentials and income potential.

Soft Skills Development: In addition to technical skills, focus on developing soft skills such as communication, leadership, and problem-solving. These skills augment your professional prowess and contribute to your overall effectiveness.

3. Networking: The Power of Connection

Networking is more than a social exercise; it is a strategic avenue to expand your influence, garner opportunities, and amplify your income-generating possibilities. Building and nurturing a strong network can open doors to collaborations, partnerships, and ventures that enhance your financial prospects.

Quality Over Quantity: Focus on building meaningful relationships rather than amassing a vast number of contacts. Engage in genuine conversations, demonstrate value, and foster mutual respect.

Industry Involvement: Participate in industry events, conferences, and professional associations. Engaging with peers, mentors, and influencers provides insights, guidance, and access to potential income-enhancing avenues.

Leveraging Digital Platforms: Leverage social media and online platforms to connect with professionals in your field. Participate in relevant online forums, LinkedIn groups, and virtual networking events to expand your reach.

In the symphony of income enhancement, the harmonious interplay of skills, education, and networking creates a melody of opportunity. By mastering these elements, you not only enrich your expertise but also pave the way for a future brimming with financial growth and prosperity.

QUOTE:

"Your pattern of success is woven from the strands of your skills, education, and networking. As you leverage these forces, you unfurl a canvas where every stroke of effort paints a masterpiece of professional growth and amplified income."

The Concept of Multiple Streams of Income and Strategies to Establish Them

Enter the realm of financial abundance through the concept of multiple streams of income – a dynamic strategy that diversifies your revenue sources and ushers in a tapestry of opportunity. Imagine your income not as a solitary stream but as a river fed by numerous tributaries, each contributing to a flourishing landscape of financial prosperity. Let's embark on a journey to unlock the potential of multiple streams of income and explore strategies to establish them:

1. Embrace the Power of Diversity: Just as a diverse investment portfolio minimizes risk, multiple streams of income shield you from the volatility of relying on a single source. This strategy thrives on variety, allowing you to tap into various avenues that resonate with your skills, interests, and market demands.

2. Leverage Your Talents: Your skills are a treasure trove of income-generating potential. Identify talents that can be monetized, whether through freelancing, consulting, teaching, or offering specialized services. Transform what you do best into a stream of earnings.

3. Venture into Entrepreneurship: Entrepreneurship offers a limitless realm of income possibilities. Launch a business aligned with your passion or address a specific market need. Online platforms, e-commerce, and innovative business models can amplify your income streams.

4. Passive Income Ventures: Passive income sources, like rental properties, royalties from creative works, or dividends from investments, generate revenue without requiring constant hands-on involvement. Cultivate assets that generate income over time, contributing to your financial stability.

5. Embrace the Gig Economy: The gig economy presents a myriad of income-generating opportunities. Engage in side gigs, freelancing, or short-term contracts that supplement your primary income and provide flexibility.

6. Invest Wisely: Investments are more than financial instruments; they are potential streams of income. Allocate resources in stocks, bonds, real estate, or mutual funds that generate dividends, interest, or capital gains, bolstering your financial inflow.

7. Digital Realm Exploration: The digital landscape offers fertile ground for income diversification. Launch a blog, podcast, YouTube channel, or online course that leverages your expertise and attracts audiences, creating a platform for monetization.

8. Rental Income and Real Estate: Investing in rental properties, commercial spaces, or real estate crowdfunding generates rental income. Real estate is a tangible asset that can provide consistent cash flow and potential appreciation over time.

9. Create Intellectual Property: Transform your knowledge into intellectual property. Write a book, develop an app, design a course, or create art that can be sold or licensed, generating royalties and passive income.

10. Collaborative Ventures: Collaboration can amplify income streams. Partner with others for joint ventures, co-authorships, or shared projects that pool resources and expertise for mutual benefit.

In weaving the tapestry of multiple streams of income, you embark on a journey of financial liberation and empowerment. The symphony of diverse revenue sources harmonizes to create a composition of stability, opportunity, and a future where your earnings flow from a myriad of sources.

QUOTE:

"In the orchestral of financial independence, each stream within the orchestra of income diversity contributes its particular song. As you establish multiple streams of income, you orchestrate a masterpiece of prosperity that resonates through the corridors of your financial journey."

Inspiring Stories of People Who Turned Their Passions into Profitable Ventures

Amidst the tapestry of entrepreneurial endeavors, there are awe-inspiring stories of individuals who kindled the flames of their passions and transformed them into profitable ventures. These tales of resilience, creativity, and unwavering dedication exemplify the remarkable potential that lies within pursuing one's passions. Let's explore a couple of these compelling stories:

1. Jane Goodall - The Conservation Crusader: Jane Goodall's unyielding passion for animals and the environment led her to a life-changing journey studying chimpanzees in Tanzania. Her pioneering research not only revolutionized our understanding of primates but also fueled her commitment to wildlife conservation. Today, the Jane Goodall Institute stands as a beacon of hope, driven by her fervent dedication to protecting endangered species and their habitats.

2. Pat Flynn - The Podcast Pioneer: Pat Flynn's passion for helping others drove him to create a blog and podcast focused on passive income and online entrepreneurship. His authentic approach and valuable content resonated with audiences, propelling him to become a leading figure in the online business space. Through his platform, Smart Passive Income, Pat not only achieved financial success but also empowered countless individuals to realize their own entrepreneurial dreams.

3. Anita Roddick - The Ethical Entrepreneur: Anita Roddick's passion for environmental sustainability and social activism led her to found The Body Shop, a cosmetics company with a strong commitment to ethical practices. Her visionary approach of combining business with social and environmental responsibility redefined the corporate landscape. The Body Shop's success demonstrated that a passion for positive change can be the driving force behind a profitable and impactful enterprise.

4. Brian Chesky - The Hospitality Innovator:

Brian Chesky's passion for travel and design led him to co-found Airbnb, a platform that revolutionized the way people experience accommodations. By transforming spare rooms into temporary lodging, Brian turned his vision into a global phenomenon that not only generated substantial revenue but also fostered cultural exchange and community building.

5. Sophia Amoruso - The Fashion Maven:

Sophia Amoruso's love for vintage clothing and a creative spirit led her to start an eBay store selling curated fashion pieces. Her dedication to curating unique, stylish items eventually evolved into Nasty Gal, a thriving fashion empire. Sophia's journey from an eBay shop to a multimillion-dollar fashion brand is a testament to the power of channeling passion into a profitable venture.

6. Elon Musk - The Innovator Extraordinaire:

Elon Musk's passion for space exploration, renewable energy, and technological innovation has driven him to establish companies like SpaceX, Tesla, and SolarCity. Musk's unwavering commitment to pushing the boundaries of human achievement has not only yielded revolutionary advancements but has also generated substantial financial success across multiple industries.

These stories illuminate the transformative potential of turning passions into profitable ventures. They serve as a reminder that the pursuit of what sets your heart on fire can fuel not only personal fulfillment but also financial prosperity. By infusing your entrepreneurial journey with genuine passion, you create a powerful recipe for success that resonates far beyond the realm of traditional business endeavors.

QUOTE:

"Common people transform into remarkable visionaries via the alchemy of passion and purpose. These stories of passion-fueled ventures are a testament to the fact that when you turn your heart's fire into action, the blaze can ignite both personal fulfillment and financial triumph."

Conclusion: Elevate Your Earning Potential

As you embark on the journey of implementing The Income Accelerator Formula, remember that the landscape of financial success is enriched by the variety and vibrancy of your income streams. By nurturing each stream with care, innovation, and dedication, you transform the pursuit of financial freedom into a symphony of prosperity.

In the upcoming chapters, we will delve into the remaining formulas that, when combined with The Income Accelerator Formula, culminate in an orchestration of wealth-building mastery. You possess the conductor's baton, poised to lead the harmonious crescendo of financial abundance.

QUOTE:

"The opportunity to enhance your financial anthem is contained inside the harmony of your talents. As you master the art of income acceleration, each note of innovation and endeavor contributes to the melody of prosperity."

THE EXPENSE MINIMIZER FORMULA
Trim Your Financial Fat

In the grand tapestry of financial mastery, prudent management of expenses stands as a cornerstone of lasting prosperity. Welcome to the Fourth Formula of "9 Formulas for Financial Freedom: Mastering Money Management and Wealth Building" – The Expense Minimizer Formula. Within these pages, we embark on a transformative journey to sculpt a leaner, more efficient financial landscape by trimming excess and optimizing every dollar spent.

The Art of Financial Sculpting

Picture your finances as a sculpture, meticulously carved to reveal its inherent beauty. The Expense Minimizer Formula is your chisel, enabling you to chip away at wasteful spending and carve out a masterpiece of financial health. This formula transcends frugality; it is a strategic approach to making mindful choices that preserve resources and foster sustainable growth.

Navigating the Path to Efficiency

Step 1: Illuminate Your Financial Landscape

Begin by shedding light on your financial landscape. Analyze your expenses with a discerning eye, categorizing them into essential needs, discretionary wants, and areas of potential reduction.

Step 2: Distinguish Between Needs and Wants

Draw a clear line between needs and wants. Differentiate between essential expenses like housing, food, and utilities and discretionary spending on non-essential items.

Step 3: Embrace the Power of Budgeting

Craft a comprehensive budget that allocates funds to each expense category. A budget is your compass, guiding you toward responsible spending while pinpointing areas for potential cutbacks.

Step 4: Audit Subscriptions and Services

Review your subscriptions, memberships, and recurring services. Assess their value and relevance; cancel or renegotiate those that no longer align with your goals.

Step 5: Implement Cost-Saving Measures

Infuse your daily routine with cost-saving strategies. Opt for energy-efficient practices, shop strategically, dine out judiciously, and seek discounts and deals whenever possible.

Step 6: Minimize Debt Burden

Prioritize debt reduction by paying off high-interest obligations systematically. Lowering your debt burden liberates financial resources that can be redirected toward wealth-building endeavors.

Step 7: Evaluate Large Purchases Thoughtfully

Before significant expenditures, adopt a deliberate approach. Research, compare prices, and consider alternatives. Taking time to evaluate prevents impulse spending and cultivates financial prudence.

Step 8: Automate Savings

Set up recurring deposits to your investment and savings accounts. recurring deposits ensures consistency and fosters a habit of setting aside funds for future growth.

The Significance of Managing Expenses and Avoiding Overspending

In the grand tapestry of financial well-being, the art of managing expenses and steering clear of the treacherous waters of overspending emerges as a foundational pillar. This fundamental practice, often underestimated, is a testament to prudent stewardship and a key to unlocking the doors of enduring financial stability. Let's delve into the significance of this art and the transformative impact it can have on your journey toward prosperity:

1. Preserving Financial Resources: Managing expenses acts as a vigilant guardian of your financial resources. By diligently monitoring where your hard-earned money flows, you ensure that each dollar is allocated purposefully and strategically. This preservation safeguards your capital, fortifying your financial foundation against unnecessary erosion.

2. Empowering Financial Goals: Every dollar saved from prudent expense management becomes a tool for advancing your financial aspirations. Whether it's building an emergency fund, investing for the future, or pursuing a lifelong dream, the discipline of managing expenses empowers you to channel resources toward your most cherished goals.

3. Mitigating Debt Burden: Overspending often paves the path to debt accumulation. Mindful expense management is a shield against this burden. By avoiding excessive spending, you mitigate the risk of falling into the cycle of debt, freeing yourself from the weight of high-interest obligations.

4. Cultivating Financial Discipline: The practice of managing expenses fosters a habit of financial discipline. It encourages you to evaluate each purchase thoughtfully, weigh its value, and align it with your priorities. This discipline extends beyond financial decisions, positively influencing other areas of your life.

5. Navigating Economic Uncertainty: In times of economic volatility or unexpected challenges, the ability to manage expenses becomes a lifeline. An established habit of prudent spending equips you with the resilience to weather storms, ensuring that your financial ship remains steady amid turbulent waters.

6. Fostering Peace of Mind: The avoidance of overspending brings a sense of tranquility to your financial landscape. The knowledge that your financial resources are managed wisely offers peace of mind, freeing you from the anxiety that accompanies reckless financial behavior.

7. Getting Financial Freedom: The key to opening the doors to financial independence is managing spending. As you curate a lifestyle that aligns with your means and values, you liberate yourself from the shackles of consumerism, enabling you to experience genuine freedom in your financial choices.

In the grand tapestry of financial well-being, the prudent management of expenses and the avoidance of overspending form a symphony of fiscal responsibility. This harmonious orchestration empowers you to sculpt a financial reality where resources are optimized, dreams are realized, and the journey to prosperity is embarked upon with purpose and intention.

QUOTE:

"The refrain of judicious spending resounds with the promise of a peaceful life amid the financial symphony. Each note of mindful expense management is a melody that contributes to the composition of financial freedom."

Practical Tips for Cutting Unnecessary Costs and Living Within One's Means

Navigating the labyrinth of financial prudence calls for a set of practical strategies that enable you to trim unnecessary costs and gracefully live within your means. These actionable tips empower you to wield the tools of fiscal efficiency, forging a path toward a balanced and sustainable financial journey. Let's delve into these pragmatic measures that empower you to master the art of living within your means:

1. Craft a Comprehensive Budget: Begin your journey by crafting a detailed budget that outlines your income, expenses, and financial goals. A well-structured budget serves as your roadmap, shedding light on areas where expenses can be trimmed and resources allocated wisely.

2. Prioritize Needs Over Wants: Distinguish between needs and wants with clarity. Prioritize essential expenses like housing, utilities, and groceries, while evaluating discretionary spending with a discerning eye. Cultivate a mindset that distinguishes between essential and non-essential purchases.

3. Track and Analyze Spending: Maintain a record of your spending habits to identify patterns and pinpoint areas of potential cutbacks. Digital tools, expense tracking apps, or even a simple notebook can help you gain insights into where your money is going.

4. Embrace Frugality Mindfully: Embrace frugality as a conscious choice. Seek cost-effective alternatives without sacrificing quality or satisfaction. Explore thrift stores, cook meals at home, or leverage discounts and coupons to maximize the value of your expenditures.

5. Minimize Impulse Spending: Before making a purchase, implement a waiting period. This practice curbs impulse spending and gives you time to evaluate whether the item is truly necessary or aligned with your financial goals.

6. Review Subscriptions and Memberships: Regularly review your subscriptions, memberships, and recurring expenses. Cancel or adjust those that no longer serve a meaningful purpose or do not align with your current priorities.

7. Reduce Utility and Energy Costs: Implement energy-saving practices to reduce utility bills. Simple steps like using energy-efficient appliances, unplugging devices when not in use, and properly insulating your home can lead to substantial cost savings.

8. Negotiate and Seek Discounts: Negotiation is a powerful tool in managing expenses. When making significant purchases or renewing contracts, don't hesitate to negotiate for better terms or seek out discounts that can help you secure a more favorable deal.

9. Automate Savings: Set up automated transfers to a dedicated savings account. Treating savings as a non-negotiable expense ensures that you consistently allocate funds toward your financial goals before discretionary spending.

10. Practice Mindful Spending: Before making a purchase, ask yourself whether it aligns with your values, goals, and long-term vision. Mindful spending cultivates awareness and helps you make intentional choices that are in harmony with your financial well-being.

By weaving these practical tips into your daily financial fabric, you embark on a journey of prudent resource allocation and intentional living. Each small action becomes a brushstroke on the canvas of financial responsibility, creating a masterpiece of balanced living and empowered choices.

QUOTE:

"In the realm of financial wisdom, the art of living within your means is a symphony of empowerment. Each choice to curtail excess is a note that contributes to the melody of fiscal harmony and the crescendo of enduring prosperity."

The Importance of Distinguishing Between Assets and Liabilities

In the intricate tapestry of financial literacy, the ability to discern between assets and liabilities emerges as a compass that guides your journey toward lasting prosperity. This fundamental distinction is a cornerstone of prudent financial decision-making, laying the groundwork for wealth accumulation and sustainable growth. Let's delve into the significance of this delineation and explore how it shapes your financial landscape:

1. Foundations of Financial Understanding: Distinguishing between assets and liabilities forms the bedrock of financial comprehension. This awareness empowers you to navigate the complexities of personal finance with clarity, enabling informed choices that align with your goals.

2. Maximizing Wealth-Building: Assets are the seeds of wealth, while liabilities can erode your financial foundation. By identifying and acquiring income-generating assets, such as investments, real estate, or business ventures, you cultivate avenues that amplify your resources over time, paving the way for wealth accumulation.

3. Mitigating Debt and Risk: Recognizing liabilities shields you from the pitfalls of debt accumulation. Managing and reducing liabilities ensures that you minimize financial risk, liberating your resources from the burden of high-interest obligations.

4. Strategic Resource Allocation: Distinguishing between assets and liabilities facilitates strategic resource allocation. You can channel your financial reserves toward acquiring appreciating assets that contribute to your net worth, rather than expending resources on depreciating liabilities.

5. Long-Term Financial Security: Assets are the building blocks of long-term financial security. The accumulation of income-generating assets, such as investments that yield dividends or rental properties that provide passive income, fortifies your financial fortress and enhances your ability to weather economic fluctuations.

6. Empowerment in Decision-Making: Clarity in discerning assets from liabilities empowers you in every financial decision. It influences choices related to major purchases, investments, debt management, and lifestyle, enabling you to align your actions with your overarching financial objectives.

7. A Catalyst for Financial Growth: Assets fuel financial growth by serving as the engine that propels your net worth forward. The more assets you accumulate, the greater your capacity to leverage opportunities, reinvest, and expand your wealth-building endeavors.

8. Legacy and Generational Impact: The cultivation of assets carries forward a legacy of financial wisdom. By imparting the importance of asset accumulation to future generations, you empower your heirs with the tools to make informed financial choices that perpetuate family prosperity.

In the grand symphony of fiscal acumen, the act of distinguishing between assets and liabilities is the conductor's baton that orchestrates a harmonious financial composition. This distinction shapes your financial canvas, allowing you to paint strokes of abundance, secure stability, and sculpt a legacy of enduring prosperity.

QUOTE:

"Within the realms of assets and liabilities lies the power to compose your financial destiny. As you master the art of discernment, each choice becomes a note that contributes to the symphony of wealth creation, playing a melody of empowerment and abundance."

Real-Life Examples of Individuals Who

Achieved Financial Freedom by Adopting a Frugal Lifestyle

In the gallery of financial success stories, there are remarkable individuals who have forged their path to freedom by embracing a frugal lifestyle. Their journeys serve as a testament to the transformative power of mindful spending, resourcefulness, and disciplined financial choices. Let's explore a few of these inspiring narratives that illuminate the art of achieving financial freedom through frugality:

1. Warren Buffett - The Sage of Saving: Warren Buffett, one of the world's most renowned investors, is celebrated not only for his astute financial decisions but also for his remarkably frugal lifestyle. Despite his immense wealth, Buffett has consistently chosen to live modestly, residing in the same house he purchased in the 1950s and favoring simple pleasures over extravagant indulgences. This unwavering frugality has been a cornerstone of his journey to becoming a self-made billionaire.

2. Elizabeth Willard Thames - The Frugalwoods Blogger: Elizabeth Willard Thames and her husband, Nate, embarked on a transformative journey to embrace a frugal lifestyle and achieve financial independence. Through their blog "Frugalwoods," they chronicled their path to early retirement by making conscious decisions to cut unnecessary expenses, grow their own food, and live intentionally. Their story resonated with a global audience seeking to redefine their relationship with money and live with purpose.

3. Mr. Money Mustache - The Vanguard of Frugality: Known by his online pseudonym, Mr. Money Mustache, Pete Adeney is a trailblazer in the world of financial independence and early retirement. Through his blog, he shares his personal journey of achieving financial freedom by optimizing expenses, biking instead of driving, and prioritizing experiences over material possessions. His story has inspired a community of like-minded individuals to embrace frugality as a means to unlock financial autonomy.

4. Vicki Robin - Co-Author of "Your Money or Your Life": Vicki Robin co-authored the influential book "Your Money or Your Life," which outlines a transformative approach to money management and personal fulfillment. Her story underscores the importance of aligning spending with values and making intentional choices to cut costs, which she believes are integral to achieving financial independence and living a life of purpose.

5. Jacob Lund Fisker - The Early Retirement Pioneer: Jacob Lund Fisker, author of "Early Retirement Extreme," pioneered a movement of extreme frugality to achieve early retirement. His lifestyle choices, including minimalist living, self-sufficiency, and DIY solutions, allowed him to save a substantial portion of his income and retire at a young age. Fisker's story challenges conventional notions of consumerism and offers an alternative path to financial freedom.

These real-life examples illustrate that the pursuit of financial freedom through frugality is not a sacrifice of quality of life, but a deliberate choice to prioritize what truly matters. These individuals demonstrate that by embracing a frugal lifestyle, one can break free from the chains of excessive consumption and forge a path toward lasting financial autonomy, enabling them to live on their own terms and pursue their passions.

THE DEBT ERADICATOR FORMULA
Crush Your Debts

Welcome to a transformative formula in "9 Formulas for Financial Freedom: Mastering Money Management and Wealth Building" – The Debt Eradicator Formula. Within these pages, we embark on a journey that wields the sword of financial liberation, cutting through the chains of debt that shackle you from realizing your true potential. This formula is your battle plan, designed to empower you to crush your debts and claim victory over the burdens that hinder your financial progress.

Unveiling the Debt Battlefield

Imagine your financial landscape as a battlefield, where debts are formidable adversaries that threaten your path to prosperity. The Debt Eradicator Formula equips you with the strategies, tactics, and unwavering resolve needed to conquer this battlefield and emerge victorious.

Strategizing for Success

Step 1: Debt Assessment and Inventory

Begin by conducting a comprehensive assessment of your debts. Compile an inventory that outlines the type, amount, interest rates, and terms of each debt. This clarity serves as the foundation upon which your debt-crushing strategy is built.

Step 2: Prioritize and Strategize

Strategically prioritize your debts. Focus on high-interest obligations first, as they drain your resources most significantly. Consider debt consolidation, negotiation, or refinancing options to optimize repayment terms and minimize interest costs.

Step 3: Create a Repayment Plan

Craft a meticulous repayment plan that allocates resources to each debt category. Utilize methodologies such as the debt snowball or debt avalanche to expedite repayment. Channel any windfalls, bonuses, or extra income toward accelerating your debt payoff.

Step 4: Cut Unnecessary Expenses

Implement cost-cutting measures to redirect funds toward debt repayment. Evaluate discretionary spending, explore ways to reduce bills, and embrace frugality as a potent weapon in your debt eradication arsenal.

Step 5: Boost Income Streams

Leverage the Income Accelerator Formula (Chapter 3) to augment your earning potential. The additional income generated can be channeled directly toward debt repayment, propelling your progress with greater momentum.

Step 6: Monitor Progress and Stay Resilient

Keep a close eye on your development and recognize each victory. The journey to debt freedom requires perseverance and resilience. Stay focused on your ultimate goal and resist the allure of unnecessary spending.

Conclusion: Crushing Debt, Emerging Triumphant

As you immerse yourself in The Debt Eradicator Formula, envision each step as a stride forward on the path to financial liberation. The battles you wage against debt are not only strategic maneuvers; they are declarations of your determination to rewrite your financial narrative.

In the chapters that follow, the symphony of formulas harmonizes to cultivate an orchestra of financial mastery. The Debt Eradicator Formula stands as a testament to your courage and commitment, fortifying your resolve to conquer debts and sculpt a future unfettered by financial burdens.

The Impact of Debt On Financial Freedom

Within the intricate framework of financial freedom, the weight of debt casts a significant shadow that can hinder progress and impede the realization of one's aspirations. This pivotal exploration delves into the profound impact of debt on the pursuit of financial autonomy, unveiling how the burden of indebtedness can shape the trajectory of your financial journey:

1. **Shackles on Progress:** Debt can become metaphorical shackles that constrain your ability to move forward. High-interest obligations divert precious resources away from savings, investments, and wealth-building opportunities, stalling the

momentum needed to achieve lasting financial freedom.

2. Erosion of Income: Interest payments on debt act as a constant drain on your income, diverting funds that could otherwise be channeled toward investments or other wealth-building endeavors. This erosion of income can hinder your ability to amass capital and capitalize on growth opportunities.

3. Limited Flexibility: Debt can limit your financial flexibility by dictating a significant portion of your monthly cash flow toward repayment. This can hinder your capacity to respond to unexpected expenses, seize investment opportunities, or make strategic financial decisions.

4. Delayed Retirement: The burden of debt can delay retirement plans, forcing you to remain in the workforce longer than desired. As a result, your ability to enjoy the fruits of your labor and pursue personal passions may be deferred, impacting the quality of your post-retirement life.

5. Impaired Creditworthiness: Accumulating debt and struggling with repayments can tarnish your creditworthiness. A lower credit score can limit your access to favorable lending terms, hindering your ability to secure loans for investments or significant life events.

6. Psychological Stress: Debt-induced stress can infiltrate various facets of life, impacting mental and emotional well-being. The weight of debt can lead to anxiety, strain relationships, and compromise overall quality of life, further challenging your pursuit of financial freedom.

7. Opportunity Costs: Every dollar directed toward debt repayment is a dollar that could have been invested or utilized to enhance your financial position. The opportunity costs of debt include missed chances to capitalize on wealth-building opportunities.

8. Hindered Wealth Accumulation: Debt diverts resources that could otherwise be allocated to savings and investments, hampering your ability to accumulate wealth. The longer debt lingers, the more it inhibits the compounding effect that fuels wealth growth.

9. Curtailed Entrepreneurial Pursuits: For aspiring entrepreneurs, excessive debt can limit the resources available to fund new ventures or innovative projects. Debt burdens may curtail your ability to take calculated risks and capitalize on business opportunities.

10. Diminished Financial Autonomy: True financial freedom is marked by autonomy over your choices and resources. Debt can undermine this autonomy, subjecting you to external financial obligations that dictate your decisions and limit your capacity to chart your desired course.

In the tapestry of financial freedom, the impact of debt is a critical thread that weaves through your journey. By understanding its implications and taking proactive steps to manage and eradicate debt, you unfurl the sails that propel you toward the uncharted waters of lasting prosperity and self-determined financial autonomy.

QUOTE:

"Amidst the interplay of dreams and debts, the choices you make today paint the canvas of your financial future. Embrace the challenge of debt management, for within its conquest lies the liberation that paves the way to a realm of unfettered financial freedom."

Strategies to Prioritize and Eliminate High-Interest Debt

In the arena of strategic financial management, prioritizing and eliminating high-interest debt stands as a formidable battlefield where calculated maneuvers pave the way to triumphant victory. This section unveils an arsenal of strategic tactics that empower you to prioritize and eradicate high-interest debt, reclaiming your financial autonomy and forging a path toward lasting prosperity:

1. The Debt Avalanche Method: Prioritize debts by interest rate, directing extra payments toward the highest interest debt first. As you conquer the debt with the highest interest, redirect the same amount to the next highest interest debt, creating a snowball effect that accelerates your journey toward debt freedom.

2. The Debt Snowball Approach: Begin by targeting the smallest debt, regardless of interest rate. Devote extra payments to eradicating this debt swiftly. The psychological boost from eliminating a debt can fuel your motivation to tackle larger obligations, propelling you toward complete debt liberation.

3. Balance Transfer Opportunities: Leverage

balance transfer options for high-interest credit card debt. Transfer balances to a card with a lower or 0% introductory interest rate. This strategic maneuver buys you time to aggressively pay down the principal before the higher interest rate kicks in.

4. Debt Consolidation Loans: Consider consolidating high-interest debts into a single, lower-interest loan. This streamlines your repayments and can reduce the overall interest burden, making it easier to manage and accelerate your debt payoff.

5. Negotiation with Creditors: Initiate conversations with creditors to negotiate better repayment terms, lower interest rates, or even settlements. Creditors may be willing to work with you to alleviate the burden and facilitate faster debt repayment.

6. Windfalls and Bonuses: Apply unexpected windfalls, tax refunds, or work bonuses directly to high-interest debt. These infusions of funds can significantly accelerate your debt reduction and expedite your path toward financial liberation.

7. Lifestyle Adjustments: Temporarily modify your lifestyle to direct more funds toward debt repayment. Cut discretionary spending, reduce entertainment expenses, and adopt a frugal approach to channel additional resources toward debt elimination.

8. Reworking Budget Priorities: Review your budget and reallocate funds previously directed toward non-essential expenditures to high-interest debt repayment. Prioritize your financial well-being by shifting resources from wants to essential debt reduction.

9. Side Gigs and Additional Income: Explore supplementary income sources, such as freelancing, consulting, or part-time work. Devote the extra earnings exclusively to high-interest debt repayment, amplifying your ability to expedite the process.

10. Consistent Monitoring and Accountability:

Establish a system to monitor your progress and hold yourself accountable. Regularly review your debt reduction plan, track your milestones, and celebrate each victory achieved along the way.

With these strategic maneuvers in your arsenal, you march forward with unwavering determination to conquer high-interest debt. Each choice, each payment, and each step becomes a testament to your commitment to financial freedom, illuminating a path that leads you from the shadows of debt to the radiant dawn of fiscal liberation.

QUOTE:

"In the thick of the struggle between willpower and debt, your tactical decisions raise a banner of empowerment. Through calculated maneuvers, you rise as the conqueror of high-interest debt, forging a path toward the pinnacle of financial mastery."

The Concept of Good Debt Vs. Bad Debt and How to Leverage It Wisely

In the intricate landscape of borrowing and financial management, the concept of good debt and bad debt serves as a compass, guiding you toward informed decisions that can either propel your financial journey or hinder your progress. This exploration unveils the duality of debt, demystifying the realms of good and bad debt, and illuminating how to harness them judiciously to serve your long-term financial objectives.

1. Good Debt: The Strategic Investment: Good

debt embodies a calculated investment that has the potential to yield substantial returns over time. This form of debt is often associated with investments in assets that appreciate or generate income. For instance, taking out a mortgage to purchase real estate or securing a student loan to pursue education can be considered good debt. These investments have the potential to enhance your financial standing, increase your earning potential, and create a pathway to future prosperity.

Leveraging Good Debt Wisely: When utilizing good debt, ensure that the investment aligns with your long-term goals and demonstrates a clear path to positive returns. Strategically manage your debt by making timely payments and taking steps to optimize your investment's growth. By doing so, you transform debt into a tool for wealth-building and long-term financial success.

2. Bad Debt: The Eroding Liability: Bad debt,

on the other hand, encompasses borrowing for non-appreciating or non-essential purposes. This type of debt often incurs high-interest rates and does not contribute to your financial well-being or future growth. Credit card debt, payday loans, or borrowing for extravagant consumer purchases are examples of bad debt. Bad debt erodes your financial foundation, perpetuating a cycle of interest payments without the promise of meaningful returns.

Mitigating Bad Debt: To minimize bad debt, practice responsible borrowing and disciplined spending. Prioritize needs over wants and avoid the allure of instant gratification through credit. If faced with bad debt, develop a plan to aggressively repay it, focusing on the highest interest obligations first. By addressing bad debt promptly, you mitigate its adverse impact on your financial health.

3. Leveraging Debt Wisely: The key to leveraging

debt wisely lies in aligning your borrowing decisions with your overall financial strategy. Before acquiring any form of debt, assess its purpose, potential returns, and impact on your financial goals. Consider the interest rates, terms, and risks associated with the debt. Strive to strike a balance between using debt as a tool for strategic growth and avoiding the pitfalls of excessive or unnecessary borrowing.

Guiding Principles:

- **Education and Research:** Educate yourself about the nature of the debt, its terms, and the potential outcomes.

- **Future Returns:** Evaluate the potential returns or benefits the debt can offer in the long run.

- **Risk Assessment:** Analyze the associated risks, including interest rates and repayment obligations.

- **Alignment with Goals:** Ensure the debt aligns with your overarching financial goals and enhances your overall financial well-being.

In the symphony of financial choices, the distinction between good debt and bad debt harmonizes with your broader financial composition. By strategically leveraging good debt and avoiding the pitfalls of bad debt, you craft a melody that resonates with fiscal prudence, empowerment, and a roadmap to lasting prosperity.

QUOTE:

The capacity to use money wisely and strategically is a skill that can be found throughout the spectrum of debt. Just as a skilled conductor orchestrates a symphony, you, too, can orchestrate a harmonious financial composition by harnessing good debt wisely and guarding against the discordant notes of bad debt."

Individuals Who Successfully Climbed Out of Debt and Built Wealth

Within the annals of financial triumph, there are captivating stories of individuals who embarked on transformative journeys, transcending the shadows of debt to emerge as architects of their own wealth. These narratives serve as beacons of inspiration, illuminating the path from debt-stricken circumstances to the pinnacle of financial success. Let's explore a few of these remarkable stories that underscore the resilience, determination, and strategic choices that led to debt eradication and the creation of lasting wealth:

1. Dave Ramsey - From Bankruptcy to Financial Guru: Dave Ramsey, a well-known personal finance expert, experienced his own financial downfall, declaring bankruptcy in his twenties. Refusing to be defined by his past, he embarked on a journey of debt elimination and financial education. Through disciplined budgeting, strategic debt payoff, and informed investing, Ramsey not only cleared his debts but also built a multimillion-dollar empire dedicated to helping others achieve financial freedom.

2. Suze Orman - A Journey from Waitress to Wealth Expert: Suze Orman's story is a testament to the transformative power of strategic financial decisions. From her humble beginnings as a waitress, Orman forged a path toward wealth by recognizing the importance of eliminating debt and embracing a frugal lifestyle. Her story resonates with countless individuals who seek to take control of their financial destinies and rewrite their financial narratives.

3. Chris Reining - Early Retirement Achieved Through Debt Freedom: Chris Reining's journey is a beacon for those striving for early retirement. By adopting a minimalist lifestyle and aggressively paying down student loan debt, Reining paved the way for financial independence. His disciplined approach allowed him to retire at the age of 37, free from the shackles of debt and empowered to pursue his passions.

4. Lauren Greutman - Overcoming Debt and Empowering Others: Lauren Greutman's story is a testament to resilience and resourcefulness. Struggling with debt and overspending, Greutman embarked on a journey to transform her financial life. Through budgeting, cutting unnecessary expenses, and adopting a frugal mindset, she not only eliminated her family's debt but also built a successful career as a financial author and educator.

5. The Martinez Family - A Debt-Free Path to Generational Wealth: The Martinez family's story exemplifies the intergenerational impact of debt eradication. Faced with significant debt, they made conscious choices to prioritize debt repayment and financial education. Their dedication not only led to debt freedom but also laid the foundation for generational wealth, as they passed down valuable financial lessons to their children.

These stories of triumph are a testament to the transformative power of strategic financial decisions. They highlight the potential for anyone, regardless of their starting point, to break free from the cycle of debt and create a legacy of lasting wealth. Through resilience, determination, and informed choices, these individuals have carved their paths to financial freedom, inspiring others to embark on their own journeys toward prosperity.

QUOTE:

"In the fabric of financial success, the tales of those who overcame crippling debt and erected castles of fortune serve as a monument to the strength of the human spirit and tactical foresight. Their narratives echo the possibilities that await each of us as we take deliberate steps toward a future illuminated by the light of financial liberation."

THE INVESTMENT MAESTRO FORMULA
Grow Your Wealth

Welcome to a Formula that unveils the realm of opportunities where your financial seeds germinate and flourish into the forest of prosperity. "The Investment Maestro Formula" is your guide to navigating the complex landscape of investments, arming you with the knowledge and strategies needed to cultivate your wealth and orchestrate a symphony of financial growth.

The Prelude: Understanding the Investment Symphony

Before we dive into the intricacies of investment strategies, it's essential to grasp the fundamental principles that underscore the art of growing your wealth. This prelude sets the stage for your journey toward becoming an investment maestro:

1. The Power of Compound Growth: Understand the magical phenomenon of compound interest, where your money earns returns on both the initial investment and the accumulated interest. This compounding effect can turn even modest investments into substantial wealth over time.

2. Risk and Reward: Balancing the Equation: Recognize that all investments carry an element of risk. However, higher potential returns often accompany higher risks. Learn how to strike a balance between risk and reward by diversifying your investment portfolio and aligning your risk tolerance with your financial goals.

3. Education as Your Baton: Empower yourself with knowledge. Learn about the various financial instruments, markets, and strategies. The more you understand, the more confidently you can wield the baton of investment decisions, directing your financial symphony toward success.

The Crescendo: Strategies for Wealth Growth

1. Stock Market Mastery: Delve into the world of stocks, where you become a conductor of companies and industries. Learn how to research, analyze, and select stocks that align with your financial objectives. Embrace a long-term perspective, harnessing the potential of equities to drive your wealth growth.

2. Bonds and Fixed Income: Explore the harmonies of bonds and fixed income securities. Understand how they provide stability and regular income to your portfolio. Learn to differentiate between government bonds, corporate bonds, and other fixed-income options to curate a balanced investment ensemble.

3. Real Estate Rhythms: Enter the realm of real estate, where properties become your instruments of wealth creation. Discover the nuances of rental properties, real estate investment trusts (REITs), and property flipping. Master the art of real estate investing to add a resonant chord to your financial composition.

4. Diversification Dynamics: Embrace the conductor's baton of diversification, spreading your investments across different asset classes and sectors. This dynamic approach mitigates risk and enhances your potential for consistent, long-term wealth growth.

5. Mutual Funds and ETFs: Conductor, meet the ensemble. Explore the world of mutual funds and exchange-traded funds (ETFs), where you invest in a diverse portfolio of assets managed by professionals. Understand the benefits of these instruments and their role in your investment symphony.

The Finale: Orchestrating Financial Symphony

As you embark on the journey of The Investment

Maestro Formula, remember that every choice, every investment decision, is a note that contributes to your financial symphony. By aligning your investments with your goals, embracing knowledge, and staying attuned to market dynamics, you become the maestro of your wealth composition. Your symphony crescendos into a harmonious composition of financial growth, echoing the triumphant finale of a life well-invested.

QUOTE:

"Within the cadence of investment decisions lies the melody of wealth growth. Each choice you make is a stroke of the conductor's baton, orchestrating a symphony of financial prosperity that resonates through the corridors of time."

Introduction to The World of Investing and Its Role in Wealth Creation

Embarking on the journey toward financial mastery

unveils a captivating realm that resonates with potential and opportunity – the world of investing. At its essence, investing is the art of deploying your financial resources strategically to cultivate growth, nurture prosperity, and orchestrate a symphony of wealth creation. This introduction illuminates the multifaceted role of investing in your quest for lasting financial freedom:

1. The Canvas of Wealth Creation: Investing serves as the canvas upon which the strokes of financial growth are painted. It empowers you to transform your hard-earned money into a dynamic force that works tirelessly to amplify your resources over time. Just as a skilled artist layers' colors to create a masterpiece, investing layers' potential returns to craft a tapestry of wealth.

2. Amplifying Financial Resources: At its core, investing magnifies your financial resources beyond the limits of saving alone. By strategically deploying funds into various investment vehicles, you harness the power of compound growth, where your money not only earns returns on its initial value but also on the accumulated interest an exponential phenomenon that fuels wealth expansion.

3. Diversification as a Shield: Investing allows you to diversify your financial portfolio, mitigating risk and increasing resilience. As you allocate funds across different asset classes, industries, and geographic regions, you create a shield that safeguards your wealth against the ebbs and flows of individual markets or economic fluctuations.

4. Navigating Inflation's Currents: Investing is a compass that guides you through the currents of inflation. Because of inflation, money loses some of its purchasing power over time. Investing offers the potential to outpace inflation, preserving and growing your wealth in a manner that safeguards your financial stability and long-term goals.

5. The Bridge to Financial Goals: Whether it's early retirement, a dream home, funding education, or leaving a legacy, investing serves as the bridge that transforms aspirations into reality. By strategically aligning your investments with your goals, you navigate the path toward achieving milestones that enhance your quality of life and shape your financial legacy.

6. The Symphony of Decision-Making: Investing is a symphony of informed decision-making, where each choice resonates with potential outcomes. It empowers you to research, analyze, and select investment opportunities that align with your risk tolerance and financial aspirations. Just as a conductor orchestrates a symphony, you conduct the ensemble of your investments to create a harmonious financial composition.

7. Cultivating Financial Education: As you explore the world of investing, you embark on a journey of continuous learning. The pursuit of investment knowledge sharpens your financial acumen, enabling you to make informed choices that optimize your returns and align with your long-term objectives.

In the grand tapestry of financial empowerment, investing emerges as a brushstroke of strategic genius, a catalyst that transforms financial resources into a dynamic force that amplifies your potential. With each investment, you wield the baton of progress, conducting the symphony of wealth creation that resonates through time, shaping a future imbued with prosperity and purpose.

QUOTE:

"Amid the mosaic of financial possibilities, investing stands as the art that turns dreams into reality. As you step onto the stage of investment, each decision becomes a note, harmonizing the melody of your aspirations into a symphony of lasting wealth."

Break Down Various Investment Options, Including Stocks, Real Estate, And Entrepreneurship

Diving into the realm of wealth creation, we embark on a journey through the labyrinth of investment options, each a unique avenue that holds the promise of financial growth and prosperity. Let's break down some of the key investment options, unveiling their intricacies and potential contributions to your wealth-building symphony:

1. Stocks: Unveiling Ownership in Companies:

Investing in stocks bestows upon you a share of

ownership in companies. By purchasing shares, you become a shareholder, participating in the company's profits and losses. Stocks offer the potential for capital appreciation and dividends, making them a cornerstone of many investment portfolios. Their liquidity and the variety of industries they encompass provide a dynamic canvas for wealth growth.

2. Real Estate: Navigating the Property Path: Real estate investing involves acquiring properties with the intent to generate income or achieve capital appreciation. Rental properties offer a steady stream of income, while property value appreciation can amplify your initial investment. Real estate investment trusts (REITs) provide a vehicle to invest in real estate without direct property ownership, further diversifying your portfolio.

3. Entrepreneurship: Forging Your Path of

Innovation: Entrepreneurship is a venture that merges passion, innovation, and strategic vision. Building your own business empowers you to create value, generate income, and potentially achieve significant returns. While entrepreneurship entails risk and requires dedication, it offers the possibility of substantial rewards and the satisfaction of realizing your vision.

4. Mutual Funds and ETFs: Collective Investment Harmony: Mutual funds and exchange-traded funds (ETFs) pool funds from multiple investors to invest in a diversified portfolio of assets. These investment vehicles offer instant diversification, allowing you to access a range of assets without the need for individual selection. They are managed by professionals who allocate funds strategically to optimize returns.

5. Bonds: Weaving the Fabric of Fixed Income:

Bonds represent debt securities issued by governments or corporations. When you invest in bonds, you essentially lend money to the issuer in exchange for periodic interest payments and the return of your principal upon maturity. Bonds provide stability and consistent income, making them an essential component of a well-balanced investment strategy.

6. Precious Metals: Safeguarding Value Beyond Currency: Investing in precious metals, such as gold and silver, offers a tangible asset that historically holds value. Inflation and economic uncertainty can be protected from with the help of precious metals. While they may not generate income like other investments, they provide a store of value and diversification.

7. Savings and CDs: Fortifying Your Financial Foundation: While not as high-yielding as other investments, savings accounts and certificates of deposit (CDs) offer a safe and secure avenue for preserving capital. They serve as a foundation for emergency funds and short-term financial goals.

As you navigate the intricate web of investment options, consider your risk tolerance, time horizon, and financial goals. Each investment avenue has its own nuances, potential returns, and associated risks. By strategically allocating your resources across different investments, you sculpt a diversified portfolio that harmonizes risk and reward, playing a symphony of financial growth that resonates with your unique aspirations.

Developing a Long-Term Investment Strategy and Managing Risk

In the labyrinth of investment endeavors, crafting a robust long-term investment strategy emerges as a beacon that guides your financial ship through the ever-shifting tides of opportunity and uncertainty. This section illuminates the art of designing a strategic investment blueprint and navigating the waters of risk management, ensuring your financial journey is characterized by stability, growth, and resilience.

1. Visionary Blueprint: A long-term investment strategy is a visionary blueprint that aligns your financial goals with a roadmap for achieving them. Begin by clarifying your objectives – whether it's retirement, wealth accumulation, or legacy planning. Define your investment horizon and risk tolerance, establishing the time frame within which your investments will mature.

2. Asset Allocation: The Composer's Symphony: Asset allocation is the composer's symphony, orchestrating a harmonious blend of different investment categories. Diversify your portfolio across various asset classes, such as stocks, bonds, real estate, and more. The strategic mix depends on your goals and risk tolerance, each component playing a distinct role in your wealth composition.

3. Risk and Return Balancing Act: Every investment journey sails on the seesaw of risk and return. Understand that higher potential returns are often accompanied by elevated risk. Strive to strike a balance that aligns with your comfort level — a blend that safeguards your capital while enabling it to flourish over time.

4. Dollar-Cost Averaging: Consistency Amidst Volatility: Implement dollar-cost averaging as your conductor's baton, ensuring consistency in your investment journey. You can buy more shares when prices are low and fewer shares when prices are high by investing a fixed sum at regular intervals. This systematic approach mitigates the impact of market volatility on your overall investment performance.

5. Patience and Discipline: The Maestro's Baton: Patience and discipline are the maestro's baton that guides your investment symphony. Avoid succumbing to emotional impulses during market fluctuations. Stay committed to your long-term strategy, allowing your investments the time to weather short-term storms and capitalize on long-term growth opportunities.

6. Periodic Review and Adjustments: The Conductor's Ear: Just as a conductor listens attentively to the orchestra, regularly review your investment portfolio. Over time, your financial situation, goals, and market conditions may evolve. Adjust your portfolio as needed to ensure it remains aligned with your objectives and reflects your changing circumstances.

7. Risk Management Ensemble: Risk management is your ensemble of safeguards that shields your portfolio from unexpected shocks. Be sure to diversify both inside and across asset groups. Explore risk mitigation tools, such as stop-loss orders, that automatically trigger sales if an investment's value drops to a certain level.

8. Professional Guidance: The Mentor's Baton:

Seek the expertise of financial professionals who serve as mentors in your investment journey. Financial advisors can offer insights, craft personalized strategies, and provide objective guidance that empowers you to make well-informed decisions aligned with your goals.

A long-term investment strategy is your symphony's overture, a carefully composed opus that guides your financial journey toward crescendos of prosperity. By harmonizing your goals, asset allocation, risk management, and unwavering discipline, you conduct a symphony that resonates with the melody of wealth growth and the assurance of a well-directed financial future.

Success Stories of Individuals Who Built Substantial Wealth Through Strategic Investments

Amid the vast expanse of financial landscapes, there stand luminous tales of individuals who embarked on transformative investment journeys, weaving a tapestry of strategic decisions that led them from humble beginnings to the zenith of substantial wealth. These stories bear witness to the power of informed choices, patient perseverance, and the orchestration of a well-crafted investment symphony. Let's delve into a few of these remarkable narratives that illuminate the path to substantial wealth through strategic investments:

1. Warren Buffett: The Oracle of Omaha's Wisdom: The name Warren Buffett is synonymous with astute investment prowess. Starting with a paper route in his youth, Buffett embarked on a journey that led him to become one of the world's wealthiest individuals. His adherence to value investing principles and his ability to identify undervalued companies propelled him to accumulate substantial wealth through his holding company, Berkshire Hathaway.

2. Ray Dalio: Bridgewater's Investment Architect: Ray Dalio's story is one of perseverance and innovation. As the founder of Bridgewater Associates, one of the world's largest hedge funds, Dalio harnessed a systematic investment approach and principles of diversification to achieve remarkable success. His dedication to rigorous research and analysis laid the foundation for his substantial wealth and the transformation of Bridgewater into an investment powerhouse.

3. John Bogle: Vanguard's Vanguard: John Bogle revolutionized the investment landscape through the creation of index funds. His belief in low-cost, passive investing and his commitment to putting investors' interests first disrupted traditional investment models. Bogle's brainchild, The Vanguard Group, grew into a behemoth, providing individuals with access to diversified investments and contributing to his own considerable wealth.

4. Sara Blakely: Spanx's Shrewd Strategist: Sara Blakely's journey from selling fax machines to becoming the youngest self-made female billionaire underscores the entrepreneurial spirit of strategic investments. As the founder of Spanx, Blakely recognized an untapped market and leveraged her innovative shapewear concept to create a global brand. Her strategic decisions and dedication to her vision translated into substantial wealth and empowerment.

5. Elon Musk: The Visionary of Diverse Ventures: Elon Musk's trajectory is a testament to audacious vision and calculated risks. From co-founding PayPal to spearheading Tesla, SpaceX, and more, Musk's strategic investments span diverse industries. His ability to anticipate market trends, harness innovation, and lead groundbreaking ventures has propelled him to remarkable wealth and global influence.

6. Abigail Johnson: Fidelity's Visionary Leader: Abigail Johnson's story is one of leadership and foresight. As the CEO of Fidelity Investments, she guided the company through strategic investments and technological advancements. Her commitment to customer-centric solutions and adaptation to evolving market trends contributed to Fidelity's growth and her own considerable wealth.

These luminous narratives unveil the remarkable transformation that stems from strategic investments. They underscore the significance of knowledge, innovation, and a calculated approach in cultivating substantial wealth. Each success story resonates as a testament to the symphony of choices that harmonize risk and reward, resilience and innovation, and ultimately, the crescendo of substantial wealth achieved through strategic investment endeavors.

In the following chapters, we delve deeper into each investment option, equipping you with the knowledge and tools needed to orchestrate a symphony of wealth creation that encompasses your vision of financial freedom.

THE TAX STRATEGIST FORMULA
Keep What You Earn

In the symphony of financial management, taxation emerges as a powerful crescendo that can either harmonize with your wealth-building efforts or create dissonance within your financial composition. "The Tax Strategist Formula" is your guide to orchestrating a melodious symphony of tax planning, ensuring you retain a harmonious portion of what you earn. This formula unveils the art of strategic tax management, enabling you to compose a financial melody that resonates with optimal tax efficiency and wealth preservation.

The Prelude: Deciphering the Tax Landscape
Before embarking on the intricate dance of tax strategies, it's essential to decode the nuances of the tax landscape. This prelude sets the stage for your journey toward becoming a tax strategist:

1. The Taxation Spectrum: Gain a comprehensive understanding of the various types of taxes that impact your financial transactions, from income tax and capital gains tax to property tax and estate tax. This knowledge forms the foundation upon which you'll craft your tax-saving symphony.

2. Tax Efficiency vs. Tax Evasion: A Moral Prelude: Embrace the ethical distinction between tax efficiency and tax evasion. While tax efficiency aims to minimize your tax liability within the boundaries of the law, tax evasion involves illegal methods to evade taxes. Your tax strategies should uphold the principles of integrity and legality.

3. Tax Planning: The Composer's Baton: Tax planning is the composer's baton that directs your financial decisions toward minimizing tax burdens. Understand how timing, income deferral, deductions, and credits play pivotal roles in orchestrating a tax-efficient composition.

4. The Tax Strategist's Toolbox: Retirement Accounts: Unveil the advantages of tax-advantaged retirement accounts such as IRAs, 401(k)s, and Roth accounts. Harness their potential to defer taxes on contributions or earnings, shaping a more harmonious tax landscape in your retirement years.

Capital Gains and Losses: Master the art of optimizing capital gains and losses to mitigate tax liabilities. Strategic selling and tax-loss harvesting are tools that can help you maintain tax efficiency within your investment portfolio.

Tax-Efficient Investments: Explore investments that offer tax advantages, such as municipal bonds, index funds, and certain life insurance policies. These instruments can compose a tax-efficient ensemble within your overall financial composition.

The Crescendo: Crafting Your Tax Symphony

1. Tailoring Strategies to Your Financial Composition: Just as a symphony is uniquely composed, tailor your tax strategies to your individual financial circumstances. Consider your income, investments, business ventures, and future goals as you craft a tax-saving symphony that resonates with your unique situation.

2. Proactive Tax Management: The Maestro's Baton: Embrace proactive tax management as the maestro's baton that guides your financial decisions. Regularly review your tax strategies and adjust them in response to changes in tax laws, financial goals, or personal circumstances.

3. Professional Harmony: Seek Guidance: Engage tax professionals – CPAs, tax advisors, or financial planners who serve as the orchestra's conductor. Their expertise ensures that your tax strategies are harmoniously orchestrated, compliant with regulations, and aligned with your wealth-building goals.

4. Legacy and Estate Planning: A Symphonic Finale: Conclude your tax-saving symphony with legacy and estate planning. Design a succession plan that optimizes wealth transfer to future generations while minimizing tax implications. A well-orchestrated estate plan ensures your financial melody endures for generations to come.

In the realm of financial empowerment, mastering the art of tax strategy becomes your virtuoso performance, allowing you to keep more of what you earn while harmonizing your financial composition with optimal tax efficiency. By conducting the symphony of tax planning, you compose a financial melody that resonates with wealth preservation, strategic decision-making, and the harmonious preservation of your hard-earned resources.

The Impact of Taxes On Financial Growth and Preservation

In the grand theater of wealth accumulation and preservation, taxes emerge as an influential character that plays a pivotal role in shaping the destiny of your financial journey. The impact of taxes is profound and far-reaching, casting its shadow on every financial transaction and decision you make. This discussion unveils the intricate interplay between taxes and your quest for financial growth and preservation, illuminating the nuances that define this complex relationship:

1. Erosion of Income: The Stealthy Thief: Taxes, often viewed as the silent thief, can erode a significant portion of your income before you even have a chance to fully embrace it. Income tax, both at the federal and state levels, siphons off a portion of your earnings, diminishing the funds available for saving, investing, and wealth accumulation.

2. Investment Impact: Dampening Returns: The impact of taxes on investments cannot be understated. Capital gains tax nibbles at the profits earned from selling assets like stocks or real estate. This dampens the overall returns on your investments, affecting your potential for wealth growth. Strategic investment choices and tax-efficient investment vehicles become vital in preserving your hard-earned gains.

3. Retirement Nest Egg: Tax-Time Realities: Even in retirement, taxes continue to exert their influence. Withdrawals from traditional retirement accounts, such as 401(k)s and IRAs, are often subject to income tax. This can potentially lower your retirement income and affect the lifestyle you've envisioned during your golden years.

4. Estate Planning: Taxing Legacy Transfer: The transfer of wealth from one generation to the next is another arena where taxes leave their mark. Estate taxes can diminish the size of the inheritance you intend to pass on to your heirs. Careful estate planning becomes essential to minimize tax implications and ensure a smooth transfer of assets.

5. Strategies for Preservation: The Shield of Planning: While taxes are a constant presence, strategic planning can act as a shield against their erosive effects. Utilizing tax-advantaged accounts, diversifying your investments, and adopting a tax-efficient investment strategy can help preserve your wealth and minimize the negative impact of taxes.

6. Tax-Efficient Investing: A Path to Preservation: Tax-efficient investing focuses on structuring your investment portfolio to minimize taxable events. This can involve holding investments for the long term to qualify for lower capital gains rates, strategically allocating assets to tax-advantaged accounts, and utilizing tax-efficient investment vehicles.

7. Tax-Loss Harvesting: Minimizing Capital Gains: Tax-loss harvesting involves deliberately selling investments that have incurred losses to offset capital gains and reduce your taxable income. This tactical approach can potentially enhance your after-tax returns and safeguard your wealth from unnecessary taxation.

In the symphony of financial growth and preservation, taxes play a central role, their melodies intertwining with every note of your financial journey. Understanding the impact of taxes empowers you to orchestrate a composition that harmonizes with your goals. By implementing strategic planning, tax-efficient investing, and prudent decision-making, you conduct a financial symphony that resonates with growth, preservation, and the fortitude to navigate the complexities of taxation while preserving the harmonious melody of your wealth.

Strategies for Optimizing Tax Efficiency, Tax-Advantaged Accounts and Deductions

Unlocking the realm of tax efficiency is akin to wielding a finely tuned instrument that can compose a harmonious melody of financial preservation and growth. Within this domain lie strategic orchestrations that allow you to navigate the intricacies of taxation while preserving more of your hard-earned resources. Here, we unveil a symphony of strategies that encompass tax-advantaged accounts and deductions, guiding you toward optimal tax efficiency:

1. Tax-Advantaged Retirement Accounts: A Prelude of Preservation: Embrace the powerful symphony of tax-advantaged retirement accounts, such as Individual Retirement Accounts (IRAs), 401(k)s, and 403(b)s. These instruments allow you to contribute pre-tax income, reducing your current taxable income while deferring taxes until withdrawal during retirement. It's a prelude of preservation that not only aids in wealth accumulation but also harmonizes with your long-term financial goals.

2. Roth Accounts: The Melody of Tax-Free Growth: The Roth IRA and Roth 401(k) contribute a harmonious cadence to your tax strategy.

Although contributions are made with after-tax dollars, qualified withdrawals in retirement are entirely tax-free. This instrument orchestrates tax-free growth, providing a compelling counterpoint to traditional retirement accounts.

3. Health Savings Accounts (HSAs): A Rhapsody of Medical Savings: HSAs compose a rhapsody of medical savings, allowing you to set aside pre-tax funds for qualified medical expenses. Contributions lower your taxable income, and withdrawals for medical purposes remain tax-free. The HSA's virtuoso performance lies in its triple tax advantage a harmonious blend of tax-free contributions, growth, and withdrawals.

4. 529 Plans: The Harmonic Chorus of Education Savings: For parents and guardians seeking to harmonize education savings, 529 plans offer an enchanting chorus. These accounts provide tax-free growth when funds are used for qualified education expenses. They allow you to conduct a symphony of financial planning that resonates with both educational aspirations and tax efficiency.

5. Itemized Deductions: The Versatile Instrument Ensemble: Itemized deductions, such as mortgage interest, state and local taxes, and charitable contributions, form a versatile ensemble of tax-saving opportunities. By itemizing deductions on your tax return, you potentially reduce your taxable income, orchestrating a symphony of financial optimization that reflects your unique circumstances.

6. Tax-Loss Harvesting: A Counterpoint of Capital Gains Management: Tax-loss harvesting offers a counterpoint to capital gains management, allowing you to offset realized capital gains with capital losses. This strategic maneuver harmonizes with market fluctuations, potentially reducing your overall tax liability and preserving your investment returns.

7. Business Expenses and Deductions: The Entrepreneur's Overture: For entrepreneurs and business owners, optimizing tax efficiency involves a symphony of business expenses and deductions. Deductible business expenses, such as office supplies, travel, and equipment, compose a virtuoso overture that reduces taxable income and supports business growth.

8. Qualified Dividend and Long-Term Capital Gains Rates: The Investment Sonata: Utilize the favorable rates of qualified dividend and long-term capital gains to conduct an investment sonata that plays to your advantage. By holding investments for a specified period, you may qualify for lower tax rates on dividends and capital gains, amplifying your after-tax returns.

In the orchestra of tax efficiency, each strategy plays a distinct note that contributes to the symphony of financial preservation and growth. By strategically leveraging tax-advantaged accounts, deductions, and prudent financial planning, you compose a harmonious composition that resonates with the melody of retaining more of your earnings while optimizing your financial journey.

The Importance of Staying Informed About Tax Laws and Changes

In the ever-evolving landscape of taxation, the importance of staying informed about tax laws and changes cannot be overstated. Just as a maestro must stay attuned to the nuances of musical compositions, so too must you remain vigilant in your understanding of tax regulations. This awareness is the key that unlocks the door to preserving your wealth, optimizing your financial strategies, and orchestrating a symphony of financial success. Here, we highlight the profound significance of staying informed about tax laws and changes:

1. Conductor of Financial Symphonies: Much like a conductor guides an orchestra through intricate musical scores, staying informed about tax laws enables you to conduct your financial symphonies with finesse. This knowledge empowers you to make well-informed decisions that harmonize with the ever-changing tax landscape.

2. Maximizing Tax Efficiency: An informed understanding of tax laws is your compass for navigating the labyrinth of tax efficiency. As tax laws evolve, new opportunities for deductions, credits, and tax-advantaged accounts may arise. Staying informed ensures you capitalize on these opportunities, optimizing your tax strategy and preserving your wealth.

3. Avoiding Costly Mistakes: Tax laws are complex and subject to revisions. Staying informed helps you avoid costly errors that could lead to penalties or unnecessary tax liabilities. By understanding the latest rules and regulations, you ensure that your financial decisions align with current tax requirements.

4. Adapting to Regulatory Changes: Tax laws are not static; they evolve in response to economic, political, and social shifts. Staying informed positioned you to adapt to regulatory changes and adjust your financial strategies accordingly. Whether it's changes to tax rates, deductions, or reporting requirements, your awareness ensures your financial compositions remain harmonious.

5. Seizing Investment Opportunities: Tax laws can impact various investment decisions, from capital gains taxation to retirement account contributions. By staying informed, you seize opportunities to strategically position your investments to align with the latest tax regulations, potentially enhancing your returns.

6. Navigating Life Transitions: Life's milestones, such as marriage, homeownership, parenthood, or retirement, often come with tax implications. Staying informed helps you navigate these transitions by understanding how tax laws apply to your changing circumstances. This knowledge ensures that your financial decisions reflect the most current tax considerations.

7. Engaging in Effective Planning: Informed tax knowledge is the cornerstone of effective financial planning. By staying abreast of tax laws, you can proactively plan for the future, make informed decisions about retirement account contributions, estate planning, and more, and ensure that your financial symphony resonates with longevity and prosperity.

8. Consulting with Professionals: Staying informed empowers you to engage with tax professionals, such as CPAs or tax advisors, from a position of knowledge. Your understanding of tax laws enables more meaningful discussions, allowing you to collaborate on strategies that optimize your financial well-being.

Just as a virtuoso musician refines their craft through continuous practice and learning, your understanding of tax laws refines your financial acumen. By embracing the imperative of staying informed, you equip yourself with the tools to navigate the complexities of taxation, compose harmonious financial strategies, and orchestrate a symphony of prosperity that resounds through every stage of your financial journey.

Examples of How Savvy Tax Planning Can Significantly Impact One's Bottom Line

The art of savvy tax planning wields a transformative wand, capable of conjuring substantial impact on one's financial bottom line.

It's a virtuoso performance that harmonizes with the rhythms of tax regulations, orchestrating a symphony of savings and preservation. Here, we illuminate examples that showcase how adept tax planning can wield its magic to significantly enhance your financial composition:

1. Retirement Account Contributions: Imagine a scenario where two individuals contribute the same amount to their retirement accounts each year. However, one opts for a tax-advantaged account, such as a traditional IRA or a 401(k), while the other chooses a regular savings account. The individual utilizing tax-advantaged accounts benefits from immediate tax deductions on contributions, allowing them to lower their taxable income and potentially save thousands of dollars in taxes each year. Over time, this strategic choice leads to a substantial difference in their retirement nest eggs.

2. Capital Gains Optimization: Consider two

investors who both realize capital gains from their investments. One investor employs tax-loss harvesting, offsetting capital gains with capital losses to minimize tax liabilities. The other investor fails to utilize this strategy. The tax-conscious investor retains a larger portion of their gains, maximizing their after-tax returns and preserving more of their investment gains.

3. Homeownership Deductions: Homeownership presents an opportunity for tax savings. A homeowner who strategically utilizes mortgage interest deductions and property tax deductions can significantly reduce their taxable income. This not only lowers their current tax bill but also frees up funds that can be reinvested or used to enhance their financial well-being.

4. Business Expenses and Deductions: Entrepreneurs who meticulously track and deduct legitimate business expenses can experience a remarkable impact on their bottom line. By lowering their taxable income, they reduce their overall tax liability and retain more of their hard-earned revenue, thus fueling business growth and personal financial goals.

5. Educational Expenses: A family investing in higher education can leverage tax-efficient savings vehicles like 529 plans. By contributing to these accounts, they accumulate funds for education expenses while benefiting from tax-free growth. When used for qualified educational costs, withdrawals from these accounts remain tax-free, significantly lightening the financial burden of tuition fees.

In the grand symphony of financial management, savvy tax planning stands as a conductor that orchestrates harmony between fiscal decisions and tax regulations. The impact of such mastery reverberates through every note of your financial journey, transforming mere notes into a harmonious composition of increased savings, optimized investments, and amplified wealth. As the curtain falls on this discourse, remember the words of Benjamin Franklin: "In this world, nothing can be said to be certain, except death and taxes." However, through savvy tax planning, you possess the power to compose a symphony that mitigates the influence of the latter, leaving you to enjoy a more melodious and prosperous financial future.

THE LEGACY BUILDER FORMULA
Secure Your Family's Future

In the tapestry of financial freedom, the threads of legacy weave a narrative that transcends generations. "The Legacy Builder Formula" is your compass, guiding you to navigate the terrain of estate planning, wealth transfer, and the enduring impact you leave on your family's future. This formula unveils the art of securing your family's legacy, ensuring that your hard-earned wealth harmoniously resonates through time, forging a legacy that echoes for generations to come.

The Foundation: Crafting Your Financial Legacy

Just as a master sculptor shapes clay into a masterpiece, your legacy is an intentional creation that shapes the lives of your loved ones. Begin your journey by establishing the foundational principles of building a lasting legacy:

1. Estate Planning: The Architect's Blueprint: Estate planning is the architect's blueprint that structures the preservation and distribution of your wealth. Craft a will, establish trusts, and appoint guardians to ensure your assets are distributed according to your wishes. This foundation is the cornerstone upon which your legacy is built.

2. Beneficiary Designations: The Guiding Constellation: Designate beneficiaries for retirement accounts, insurance policies, and other assets to navigate the constellation of your legacy. These designations ensure a seamless transfer of assets and avoid potential probate hurdles, harmonizing the transition of wealth to your heirs.

3. Family Values and Philanthropy: The Moral Melody: Weave a moral melody into your legacy by imparting your family's values and encouraging philanthropy. Establishing charitable foundations or donor-advised funds resonates with a symphony of giving, leaving a positive impact on both your family and the wider community.

4. Long-Term Care and Health Care Directives: The Caring Crescendo: Your legacy encompasses not only wealth but also your health and well-being. Create long-term care plans and health care directives that harmonize with your intentions. These measures ensure that your family is equipped to make crucial decisions during times of need.

Harmonizing with the Future: Orchestrating the Legacy

1. Open Conversations: The Dialogues of Legacy: Initiate open conversations with your loved ones about your legacy plans. Discuss your wishes, explain the rationale behind your decisions, and create an environment of understanding. These dialogues form a harmonious bridge that connects your intentions with their expectations.

2. Wealth Transfer Strategies: The Inheritance Symphony: Utilize wealth transfer strategies to compose an inheritance symphony that reflects your desires. Gifting strategies, trusts, and generation-skipping techniques harmonize with tax-efficient wealth transfer, ensuring your legacy flourishes while minimizing tax burdens.

3. Education and Empowerment: The Gift of Knowledge: Empower your heirs with financial education. By imparting knowledge about managing wealth, investments, and estate planning, you equip them with the tools to continue the legacy you've crafted.

4. Review and Adaptation: The Legacy's Evolution: The legacy you build is not static; it evolves with changing circumstances. Regularly review and adapt your estate plans to reflect major life events, such as births, marriages, or significant financial changes. This ensures your legacy remains in tune with your family's needs.

The Crescendo: Leaving a Lasting Melody

Your legacy is more than material wealth; it's the symphony of your values, aspirations, and love that echoes through time. As the final notes of this chapter resound, consider the words of Maya Angelou: "I have learned that you shouldn't go through life with a catcher's mitt on both hands. You must be able to return with something. The potential to leave behind a legacy of knowledge, empowerment, and success is your legacy. Through "The Legacy Builder Formula," you orchestrate a harmonious composition that secures your family's future, ensuring that your financial symphony resonates as a lasting melody that brings harmony and prosperity to generations yet to come.

Estate Planning, Wills, Trusts, and The Importance of Protecting Assets

Estate Planning: Safeguarding Your Symphony

Estate planning, akin to composing a masterpiece, is the process of harmonizing your financial affairs to ensure a seamless transition of assets and values to future generations. Just as a conductor orchestrates every instrument to create a harmonious symphony, estate planning orchestrates your financial components to create a lasting legacy:

1. Wills: Crafting Your Melody of Intent: Your estate plan's cornerstone is a will. It outlines your wishes regarding asset distribution, guardianship of minor children, and more. Just as a composer's score guides musicians, your will guides your loved ones, ensuring your intentions are upheld and your legacy is preserved.

2. Trusts: A Melodic Structure of Control: Trusts compose a versatile ensemble within your estate plan. Revocable living trusts can help avoid probate and provide a seamless transfer of assets. Irrevocable trusts can serve as a protective shield for assets, preserving wealth for beneficiaries while minimizing estate tax liabilities.

3. Beneficiary Designations: The Harmonic Transfer: Designating beneficiaries for retirement accounts, life insurance policies, and other assets is akin to assigning instrumental roles in a symphony. These designations ensure your assets transition smoothly to your chosen heirs, bypassing probate and harmonizing with your overall estate plan.

4. Asset Protection: Safeguarding the Symphony: Just as a conductor shields delicate instruments from harm, asset protection safeguards your wealth from potential risks. Limited liability companies (LLCs), family limited partnerships (FLPs), and proper insurance coverage form a protective barrier, preserving your assets for the benefit of your heirs.

The Crescendo of Protection
1. Legacy Preservation: Ensuring Intentions Are Heard: Estate planning ensures your legacy is not left to chance. It's your opportunity to amplify your voice even when you're no longer present, orchestrating a harmonious transition of assets and values that resonates with your intentions.

2. Minimizing Conflicts: Harmonizing Family Dynamics: Proper estate planning helps mitigate potential conflicts among heirs. It addresses potential disputes by clarifying your wishes and providing a roadmap for asset distribution, fostering family unity and minimizing discord.

3. Tax Efficiency: A Strategic Symphony: Estate planning conducts a strategic symphony that harmonizes with tax regulations. It leverages legal strategies to minimize estate taxes, preserving more of your wealth for your heirs and ensuring that the crescendo of your financial legacy endures.

4. Flexibility and Adaptation: A Responsive Sonata: Estate planning is not a static composition; it's a responsive sonata that evolves with your circumstances. Regular reviews and updates ensure your legacy remains aligned with your family's needs, adapting to life's changing rhythms.

The Overture to a Lasting Legacy

As we conclude this discussion on estate planning and asset protection, let these words by Benjamin Franklin resonate: "An investment in knowledge pays the best interest." Your investment in crafting a comprehensive estate plan and safeguarding your assets is an investment in securing the best interest of your loved ones. It's the overture that paves the way for a lasting legacy – a symphony of prosperity, protection, and preservation that echoes through the corridors of time, leaving an enduring melody for generations to come.

Guidance On Passing Down Financial Wisdom and Values to The Next Generation

Just as a conductor imparts his musical expertise to the orchestra, passing down financial wisdom to the next generation is an act of empowerment that shapes their journey toward prosperity. It's a melody of guidance and knowledge that resonates through time, enriching their lives and ensuring the continuity of your legacy:

1. Open Conversations: The Prelude to Knowledge: Initiate open dialogues with your family about finances. Share your experiences, successes, and even failures. By discussing money matters openly, you create an environment of trust and understanding, laying the foundation for a harmonious financial future.

2. Teaching Financial Literacy: The Educational Score: Just as musicians learn to read music, impart financial literacy to your heirs. Teach them the fundamentals of debt management, investing, saving, and budgeting. This knowledge equips them to navigate their financial symphony with confidence.

3. Lead by Example: The Conductor's Baton: Your actions serve as a conductor's baton that directs your family's financial journey. Demonstrate responsible financial behaviors, such as living within means, making informed investments, and giving back. Your example becomes their guiding tempo.

4. Involve Them in Financial Decisions: A Collaborative Duet: Engage your heirs in financial decisions, allowing them to participate in discussions about investments, estate planning, and charitable giving. This collaborative duet fosters a sense of ownership and responsibility, empowering them to make informed choices.

Values and Legacy: Crafting a Harmonious Future
1. Define Your Family Values: The Compass of Integrity: Just as a composer sets the key signature, define your family's financial values. Emphasize principles such as stewardship, philanthropy, and responsible wealth management. These values serve as the compass that guides their financial decisions.

2. Document Your Intentions: The Score of Guidance: Put your financial intentions in writing, creating a document that outlines your values, goals, and legacy wishes. This "financial score" offers clarity and direction, ensuring that your legacy continues to resonate with your family's harmonious financial journey.

3. Encourage Independence: Orchestrating Confidence: As a conductor empowers musicians to perform solo passages, encourage financial independence among your heirs. Provide opportunities for them to manage their finances, make investment choices, and learn from real-world experiences.

4. Celebrate Milestones: Harmonizing Achievements: Just as a performance is celebrated with applause, acknowledge your heirs' financial milestones. Whether it's purchasing a first home, starting a business, or contributing to a charitable cause, celebrate their achievements and reinforce the significance of responsible financial management.

Harmony Across Generations: The Grand Finale

As we conclude this exploration of passing down financial wisdom and values, remember the words of Jim Rohn: "For every disciplined effort, there is a multiple reward." Your disciplined efforts in passing down financial wisdom and values yield a multiple reward a harmonious blend of empowerment, unity, and prosperity that reverberates through generations. Through your guidance, your family becomes the orchestra that performs your financial symphony with grace and confidence. Embrace this role with dedication, knowing that your legacy will crescendo into a melody of enduring success and harmony that transcends time.

Inspiring Stories of Individuals Who Built Lasting Legacies for Their Families and Communities.
1. Andrew Carnegie: A Philanthropic Maestro:
Andrew Carnegie, a Scottish-American industrialist and philanthropist, built a legacy that continues to impact communities worldwide. From humble beginnings, Carnegie amassed great wealth in the steel industry. However, he believed in giving back and using his fortune for the greater good. He

funded the construction of over 2,800 public libraries, contributing to education and knowledge dissemination. His philanthropic efforts laid the foundation for countless individuals to access education, inspiring generations to come.

2. Oprah Winfrey: Empowering Lives Through Media: Oprah Winfrey's rise from poverty to media mogul is a testament to determination and resilience. Her success extended beyond personal achievement as she used her platform to empower others. Through her talk show and media empire, Oprah shed light on important issues, initiated conversations, and supported causes close to her heart. Her leadership and generosity, including establishing educational foundations, have left an indelible mark on countless lives.

3. Warren Buffett: The Sage of Financial Wisdom: Warren Buffett, one of the world's most successful investors, built a legacy of financial wisdom and philanthropy. Despite his immense wealth, Buffett is known for his frugal lifestyle and commitment to charitable giving. He pledged to donate the majority of his fortune to philanthropic endeavors, notably the Bill and Melinda Gates Foundation. Buffett's approach to wealth accumulation and his dedication to helping others exemplify a harmonious blend of financial acumen and altruism.

4. Malala Yousafzai: A Voice for Education and Equality: Malala Yousafzai, a Pakistani advocate for education and women's rights, defied adversity to leave a profound legacy. Shot by the Taliban for advocating girls' education, Malala's resilience and unwavering commitment to her cause earned her global recognition. Her advocacy led to the establishment of the Malala Fund, which supports education for girls in marginalized communities. Malala's legacy is one of empowerment and the transformative power of education.

5. Bill and Melinda Gates: Pioneers of Global Philanthropy: Bill and Melinda Gates, co-founders of Microsoft, have channeled their wealth and influence to address global challenges. Through their foundation, they have focused on improving healthcare, education, and alleviating poverty worldwide. Their commitment to philanthropy and innovative solutions has saved lives, transformed communities, and demonstrated the impact that strategic giving can have on a global scale.

6. Nelson Mandela: A Legacy of Unity and Equality: Nelson Mandela, the iconic leader of the anti-apartheid movement and former President of South Africa, left an enduring legacy of unity and equality. His lifelong dedication to ending racial segregation and fostering reconciliation helped transform a nation. Mandela's commitment to justice, forgiveness, and human rights inspired a harmonious transition from oppression to democracy, leaving an indelible mark on history.

These inspiring individuals have demonstrated that building a lasting legacy goes beyond personal accomplishments. Through their actions, they have enriched the lives of others, contributed to positive change, and left a symphony of empowerment and progress that echoes through time. Their stories serve as a testament to the profound impact that intentional actions and values-driven decisions can have on families, communities, and the world at large.

THE FREEDOM ACHIEVER FORMULA

Unlocking Your Financial Independence

In the grand finale of our symphony of financial mastery, we present "The Freedom Achiever Formula." Like a crescendo that builds to a triumphant climax, this formula is a call to action, inviting you to step onto the stage of financial independence and embrace the melody of freedom. Here, we unravel the art of transforming your aspirations into reality, harmonizing discipline, perseverance, and strategic decision-making to unlock the door to your ultimate goal: complete financial freedom.

1. Conductor of Your Destiny: The Baton of Empowerment

Imagine yourself as the conductor of your financial journey, wielding the baton of empowerment. The Freedom Achiever Formula places you at the helm, guiding your fiscal decisions with purpose and intention. By assuming control, you orchestrate a composition that echoes with the harmony of self-determination.

2. Vision and Goal Setting: Crafting the Score of Success

Just as a composer envisions a musical masterpiece, articulate your financial goals with clarity. Define your aspirations, from debt elimination to retirement dreams, and craft a symphonic score that outlines the steps needed to achieve them. This vision serves as the compass that steers your financial ship toward the shores of freedom.

3. Strategic Execution: The Harmony of Action

A symphony comes to life through the execution of meticulously planned notes. Similarly, the Freedom Achiever Formula emphasizes strategic execution. It's the discipline to adhere to budgets, invest wisely, and stay on course, transforming your financial intentions into a harmonious reality.

4. Perseverance: The Resilient Rhythm

Just as a musician practices tirelessly, financial freedom demands perseverance. Embrace challenges as opportunities to refine your financial composition. When setbacks arise, remember that every note contributes to the grand symphony of your success.

5. Embracing Change: Adapting to New Tempos

The world of finance, like music, evolves over time. Embrace change and adapt to shifting rhythms. As you master the art of flexibility and adaptability, you fine-tune your financial symphony to resonate with the changing tides of economic landscapes.

The Crescendo of Freedom: Your Financial Overture

The culmination of your financial journey is the crescendo of freedom. Picture yourself stepping into the spotlight of financial independence, the culmination of the melodies you've crafted throughout this book. Your legacy of financial acumen, empowerment, and prosperity is a resounding overture that reflects the culmination of your efforts.

As you prepare to take your final bow on this journey, let the words of Robert Kiyosaki ring true: "The single most powerful asset we all have is our mind. It may produce massive wealth in what seems like an instant if properly trained. The Freedom Achiever Formula allows you to use your mind's power to create not only wealth but also the symphony of complete financial freedom. Your journey has been a crescendo of learning, empowerment, and transformation. Now, it's time to step into the spotlight and embrace the liberating melody of financial independence.

Living Your Dream Life
As the curtain rises on the final act of our financial symphony, the spotlight shifts to the most captivating melody of all: living your dream life. Just

as a composer's masterpiece is performed to captivate an audience, your journey through the Freedom Achiever Formula has been a symphony designed to lead you to this grand crescendo. Now, it's time to step into the limelight and bask in the harmony of a life that resonates with fulfillment and purpose.

1. Define Your Dream Life: The Composer's Canvas: Much like a composer selecting instruments and tones, define the elements that compose your dream life. Envision the places you want to visit, experiences you want to savor, and the sense of fulfillment you desire. This canvas becomes the backdrop against which your financial symphony is performed.

2. Financial Freedom as the Conductor: Just as a conductor guides an orchestra, your achieved financial freedom orchestrates the performance of your dream life. It affords you the autonomy to make choices aligned with your passions and values, transforming your dreams into tangible experiences.

3. Invest in Experiences: The Melody of Moments: The true richness of life lies not in possessions but in experiences. Allocate your resources to create memorable moments, whether it's traveling to far-off destinations, indulging in hobbies, or spending quality time with loved ones. These experiences compose the melodies that make your life's symphony enchanting.

4. Contributing to Others: The Harmony of Impact: Just as a musical performance resonates with the audience, contribute to the well-being of others. Engage in acts of philanthropy, volunteerism, or mentorship that harmonize with your values. The impact you create becomes a harmonious echo in the lives of those you touch.

5. Balancing Wealth and Well-Being: The Rhythm of Contentment: As a conductor balances different musical elements, harmonize your pursuit of wealth with overall well-being. Strive for balance that encompasses physical, emotional, and mental health. After all, the ultimate dream is not only financial success but also a life imbued with serenity and contentment.

The Grand Finale: Living Your Symphony
Your journey through the Freedom Achiever Formula has been an orchestration of financial empowerment and strategic decisions, culminating in the crescendo of living your dream life. Your financial symphony, conducted with precision and intention, now reaches its grand finale:

As you take your final bow in this magnificent performance, let these words by Henry David Thoreau resonate: "Go confidently in the direction of your dreams. Live the life you have imagined." Your pursuit of financial freedom and the orchestration of your dream life is a testimony to your dedication, discipline, and the power of intentional living. Embrace each note of your symphony with gratitude and enthusiasm, for you are the composer, conductor, and lead performer of a life that harmonizes with your deepest aspirations. Now, go forth with confidence and embark on the exhilarating journey of living the life you have imagined a symphony of fulfillment that will resound for generations to come.

Summaries of The Key Principles of the Formula.

Throughout the preceding formulas of "9 Formulas for Financial Freedom: Mastering Money Management and Wealth Building," a symphony of essential principles has unfolded, each contributing to the harmonious composition of financial mastery and lasting prosperity. Let's recap the key principles that have resonated through the pages of this book:

Chapter 1: The Foundation Formula - Mind Your Mindset

- The influence of mindset on financial results.

- The distinction between scarcity and abundance mindsets.

- Practical strategies to cultivate a wealth-oriented mindset.

- How a positive mindset leads to better financial decisions and opportunities?

Chapter 2: The Wealth Blueprint Formula - Design Your Financial Plan

- The significance of creating a clear financial blueprint.

- Strategies to set financial goals and achieve them.

- The importance of diversification and risk management in wealth-building.

- Examples of successful individuals with effective wealth blueprints.

Chapter 3: The Income Accelerator Formula -

Multiply Your Earnings

- The value of increasing one's earning potential.

- Leveraging skills, education, and networking to boost income.

- Introducing multiple streams of income and establishing them.

- Inspiring stories of individuals turning passions into profitable ventures.

Chapter 4: The Expense Minimizer Formula - Trim Your Financial Fat

- Addressing the significance of managing expenses and avoiding overspending.

- Practical tips for cutting unnecessary costs and living within means.

- Distinguishing between assets and liabilities.

- Real-life examples of frugal lifestyles leading to financial freedom.

Chapter 5: The Debt Eradicator Formula - Crush Your Debts

- Exploring the impact of debt on financial freedom.

- Strategies to prioritize and eliminate high-interest debt.

- Understanding good debt vs. bad debt and leveraging it wisely.

- Stories of individuals overcoming debt and building wealth.

Chapter 6: The Investment Maestro Formula - Grow Your Wealth

- Introduction to investing and its role in wealth creation.

- Different investment options, including stocks, real estate, and entrepreneurship.

- Insights into developing a long-term investment strategy and managing risk.

- Success stories of individuals building wealth through strategic investments.

Chapter 7: The Tax Strategist Formula - Keep What You Earn

- Discussing the impact of taxes on financial growth and preservation.

- Strategies for optimizing tax efficiency, including tax-advantaged accounts and deductions.

- The importance of staying informed about tax laws and changes.

- Examples of how tax planning can significantly impact one's bottom line.

Chapter 8: The Legacy Builder Formula - Secure Your Family's Future

- Crafting a financial legacy through estate planning and protecting assets.

- Passing down financial wisdom and values to the next generation.

- Inspiring stories of individuals who built lasting legacies for their families and communities.

Chapter 9: The Freedom Achiever Formula - Unlocking Your Financial Independence

- The journey to financial independence through strategic decision-making.

- Living your dream life by aligning financial freedom with personal fulfillment.

- Balancing wealth and well-being for a harmonious life.

- Embracing the power of intentional living and realizing your aspirations.

These principles compose a symphony of wisdom, guidance, and inspiration that empower you to master money management, build wealth, and orchestrate a life of lasting financial freedom. Just as each note contributes to a musical masterpiece, each principle contributes to your symphony of financial success. Embrace these principles, conduct your financial journey with purpose, and create a symphony of prosperity that reverberates through time.

The Power of Financial Freedom in Achieving Personal Dreams and Goals.

Imagine a life where your aspirations know no boundaries, where your dreams are not constrained by financial limitations, and where you have the resources to turn your deepest desires into reality. This is the transformative essence of financial freedom, the conductor of your symphony of personal dreams and goals.

Empowering Dream Realization: Financial freedom is the instrument that empowers you to compose a life aligned with your truest passions and ambitions. It liberates you from the constraints of financial stress, freeing your mind to explore uncharted territories of creativity, innovation, and self-discovery. With a firm foundation of financial security, you possess the confidence to chase your dreams without hesitation, knowing that your orchestration of resources is in perfect harmony with your aspirations.

The Canvas of Endless Possibilities: Consider financial freedom as the canvas upon which you paint the vivid tapestry of your personal dreams and goals. Just as a painter uses each brushstroke to bring a masterpiece to life, you utilize your financial freedom to craft experiences, journeys, and accomplishments that resonate with your heart's desires. Whether it's traveling the world, launching a business, pursuing advanced education, or giving back to your community, your financial freedom becomes the medium through which you express the symphony of your life.

Unleashing Creativity and Innovation: Financial

freedom is the conductor's baton that leads the orchestra of your creativity and innovation. It encourages you to explore uncharted genres, experiment with novel ideas, and take calculated risks that propel you closer to your dreams. With the weight of financial constraints lifted, you're free to compose new melodies, explore unconventional paths, and discover innovative solutions to challenges that once seemed insurmountable.

Legacy of Inspiration: Achieving personal dreams and goals through financial freedom extends beyond individual fulfillment; it becomes a legacy of inspiration for those who follow. Just as a composer's work influences generations of musicians, your pursuit of personal dreams resonates through time, encouraging others to dare, strive, and reach for their own aspirations. Your symphony of achievement becomes a testament to the boundless potential that financial freedom unlocks.

In the grand symphony of life, financial freedom is the overture that sets the tone for harmonious living. It's the crescendo that crescendos the brilliance of your dreams and goals, amplifying their impact and ensuring their enduring resonance. As you continue to conduct your financial journey with intention, remember the words of Walt Disney: "All our dreams can come true if we have the courage to pursue Accept the power of financial independence and let it direct you as you bravely work toward the symphony of your individual hopes and aspirations.

Take Action, Stay Committed, and Persevere on Your Financial Journey.

Dear reader, you have embarked on a journey through the harmonious chapters of financial mastery, and within each page lies the potential to orchestrate a life of profound prosperity and fulfillment. But remember, just as a symphony is brought to life by the musicians' dedication and precise execution, your financial journey requires action, commitment, and unwavering perseverance.

Stay Committed to Your Composition: As you traverse the path toward financial freedom, challenges may arise, and the rhythm of life may test your resolve. In these moments, hold fast to your commitment. Like a conductor guiding an orchestra through intricate passages, your commitment ensures that your financial symphony stays on course, building crescendo after crescendo of success.

Perseverance: The Key to Masterful Overtures: In the world of music, it's the hours of practice, the unwavering determination, and the relentless pursuit of excellence that transform a musician into a virtuoso. Similarly, your financial journey is a continuous process of learning, adapting, and overcoming. When faced with setbacks, let perseverance be your guide the tenacious rhythm that propels you forward even when the notes are challenging.

The Grand Finale: Your Personal Overture of Triumph: Visualize the culmination of your financial journey as the grand finale of an awe-inspiring performance. As you conquer debt, build wealth, and actualize your dreams, your symphony resounds with a melody of triumph and accomplishment. Your commitment and perseverance set the stage for this unforgettable moment – the moment when you step into the spotlight of complete financial freedom.

In the words of Helen Keller,

"Optimism is the faith that leads to achievement. Nothing can be done without hope and confidence."

As you stand at the precipice of your financial journey, remember that every note you play, every decision you make, and every action you take contributes to the composition of your financial success.

Take action with optimism, stay committed to your dreams, and let your perseverance be the cadence that propels you forward. The symphony of your financial journey is one of resilience, empowerment, and transformation. Embrace the conductor's baton, wield it with purpose, and compose a life that resonates with the harmonious echoes of financial freedom.

With hope in your heart and confidence in your stride, play on, maestro, play on. Your symphony of financial triumph awaits, and the world eagerly anticipates the masterpiece you are destined to create.

A Life of Purpose, Fulfillment, and Contribution

As we draw the final curtain on this chapter, it's not just the culmination of financial strategies and principles that we celebrate; it's the crescendo of a life well-lived, a symphony of purpose, fulfillment, and contribution. The harmony of financial freedom is not an end in itself but a gateway to a life imbued with deeper meaning and resonance.

Embrace Your Unique Composition: Just as a composer infuses their music with unique melodies, harmonies, and rhythms, you possess the power to craft a life uniquely your own. Embrace your passions, talents, and values, and let them guide your life's composition. Seek out activities, pursuits, and experiences that resonate with your heart, for it is in these moments that you create the most beautiful and impactful refrains.

Pursue Lifelong Fulfillment: Financial freedom is not solely about accumulating wealth; it's about using that wealth as a conduit to experience profound fulfillment. It's the freedom to engage in activities that ignite your soul, spend quality time with loved ones, and savor the richness of life's tapestry. Let every note of your journey be a reminder that fulfillment comes not only from what you have but from the moments you create.

Contribute to the Greater Symphony: As you stand on the stage of your life, consider the impact you have on the world around you. Just as a musician contributes to the harmonious ensemble, your actions, choices, and contributions have a ripple effect that resonates far beyond your individual sphere. Engage in acts of kindness, generosity, and service, for it is through contribution that you amplify the melody of positivity in the world.

Live Your Symphony of Impact: In the grand finale of your financial journey, remember that the symphony of your life extends far beyond your financial success. It's the symphony of moments, relationships, and experiences that you compose with intention. It's a melody of purpose-driven living, where your financial freedom becomes the backdrop against which you paint strokes of compassion, growth, and meaningful change.

As you take your final bow, let these words by Maya Angelou reverberate in your heart: "My mission in life is not merely to survive, but to thrive; and to do so with some passion, some compassion, some humor, and some style." Embrace the symphony of purpose, fulfillment, and contribution, and play your part with passion, compassion, humor, and your own unique style. Your life is the grandest composition you will ever create let it resound with the harmonious echoes of a life well-lived.

CONCLUSION

The Harmonious Crescendo of Your Journey

As we arrive at the final pages of "9 Formulas for Financial Freedom: Mastering Money Management and Wealth Building," it is with a sense of fulfillment and gratitude that we reflect on the transformative journey you, our cherished readers, have embarked upon. Just as a symphony reaches its climactic crescendo, so too does your journey through these chapters culminate in a powerful harmony of knowledge, empowerment, and aspiration.

Throughout this book, we have traversed the landscape of financial mastery, exploring the intricate notes of mindset, wealth creation, debt eradication, investment strategies, and so much more. Each chapter served as a movement in your symphony of growth, expanding your understanding, nurturing your ambition, and equipping you with the tools to shape your financial destiny.

From the inception of cultivating a wealth-oriented mindset to the poignant crescendo of living a life of purpose and contribution, you have embraced the conductor's baton and guided your financial journey with intention. You have uncovered the melodies of financial literacy, composed harmonies of prudent decision-making, and orchestrated the rhythm of perseverance.

As you turn the final pages and reflect on the orchestra of insights you've gathered, remember that this book is not just a compilation of words on paper; it's a compass that points you toward a life of abundance, fulfillment, and boundless possibility. The transformative journey you've undertaken is not confined to these pages; it echoes in your thoughts, decisions, and actions as you move forward.

While this book may come to a close, your symphony of financial empowerment continues to play on. You are the maestro of your financial journey, and the world eagerly anticipates the harmonious composition you are destined to create. As you march to the beat of your ambitions, remember the wisdom of Ralph Waldo Emerson:

"Do not go where the path may lead, go instead where there is no path and leave a trail."

Embrace the extraordinary, embrace the uncharted, and most importantly, embrace your potential to leave a trail of financial mastery, impact, and inspiration. May your symphony resound with the triumphant notes of achievement, purpose, and lasting legacy. Your transformative journey has just begun, and the melodies you compose will echo through time, inspiring generations to come.

Embracing Lifelong Learning and Adaptation

As we bid adieu to the final chapter of "9 Formulas for Financial Freedom: Mastering Money Management and Wealth Building," it is crucial to recognize that your journey doesn't culminate here. Instead, it harmoniously blends into the ongoing composition of your life — a composition that thrives on continuous learning and the ability to adapt to ever-changing financial landscapes.

Just as a skilled musician hones their craft through tireless practice and dedication, your pursuit of financial mastery is an ongoing journey that requires constant growth. The world of finance is like a symphony, evolving, shifting, and introducing new melodies with each passing day. To stay attuned and in sync, you must be committed to the pursuit of knowledge and open to adapting your strategies as the tempo of the financial world changes.

The Melody of Lifelong Learning: Knowledge

really is power in the financial world. The commitment to lifelong learning equips you with the tools to navigate the complex interplay of markets, regulations, and economic shifts. By staying informed, you empower yourself to make informed decisions, capitalize on emerging opportunities, and shield yourself from potential pitfalls.

Adapting to Changing Landscapes: Just as a symphony may shift from a serene adagio to a lively allegro, the financial landscape can change unexpectedly. Economic downturns, technological advancements, and global events can alter the rhythm of the market. Your ability to adapt and adjust your financial strategies accordingly ensures that you remain resilient in the face of uncertainty.

A Harmonious Blend of Wisdom and Flexibility: As you carry the symphonic echoes of this book with you, remember that your financial journey is a harmonious blend of wisdom and flexibility. The wisdom you've gained from these pages will serve as your foundation, while the flexibility to embrace new knowledge and adapt to change will be your guiding light.

As you continue to compose the opus of your financial life, embrace the sentiment of Henry Ford: "Anyone who stops learning is old, whether at twenty or eighty." Your journey is a perpetual crescendo, a never-ending symphony of growth and evolution. Embrace every note of discovery, every chord of adaptation, and every refrain of success, for they compose the harmonious soundtrack of a life well-lived.

So, dear reader, let your thirst for knowledge be unquenchable, your appetite for growth insatiable, and your willingness to adapt unwavering. As you navigate the financial landscapes that lie ahead, know that the symphony of your journey will continue to resonate with purpose, resilience, and the transformative power of continuous learning.

Embracing the Ever-Evolving Symphony of Financial Freedom

As you reach the final notes of "9 Formulas for Financial Freedom: Mastering Money Management and Wealth Building," it's essential to recognize that the pursuit of financial freedom is not a final destination but an ongoing symphony that resonates throughout your life. Just as a masterful composition continues to be refined and perfected, your journey toward financial freedom is an ongoing process, ripe with opportunities for growth, refinement, and new harmonies.

A Symphony of Progress and Growth: Financial freedom is not a static concept; it's a living, breathing symphony that evolves alongside your aspirations, circumstances, and achievements. The skills you've acquired, the principles you've embraced, and the mindsets you've cultivated are the building blocks of a lasting and vibrant financial future. The journey doesn't end; rather, it transforms into an exhilarating dance of progress and growth.

Celebrate Your Success, Pay It Forward: Just as a powerful melody lingers in the hearts of those who listen, your success story holds the potential to inspire and uplift others. Your journey through this book has equipped you with the tools and insights to navigate the complexities of finance and wealth-building. Now, it's your turn to be the conductor of positive change.

Share your triumphs, both large and small, with those around you. Be a beacon of inspiration and a source of guidance for friends, family, and even strangers who seek the symphony of financial freedom. By sharing your experiences, you become a conductor of hope, conducting a symphony of empowerment for others to follow.

The Melody of Paying It Forward: In the words of Anne Frank, "No one has ever become poor by giving." Your willingness to extend a helping hand, to share your wisdom and lessons learned, enriches not only the lives of others but also your own. As you help others compose their own financial symphonies, you reinforce your own understanding, strengthen your commitment, and contribute to a harmonious community of empowered individuals.

So, dear reader, as you turn the final page of this book, remember that the closing note of one chapter is but the prelude to the next. The pursuit of financial freedom is a lifelong journey, an eternal melody of growth, impact, and purpose. Share your successes, continue to learn and adapt, and let your journey inspire a symphony of positive change in the lives of those around you. In doing so, you contribute to a world where the melody of financial empowerment resounds far and wide, enriching lives for generations to come.

ABOUT THE AUTHOR

M. D. Lloyd is a distinguished financial strategist, educator, and author with a passion for empowering individuals to master money management and attain lasting financial freedom.

With a background in finance and extensive experience in wealth building, M. D. Lloyd combines a deep understanding of economic principles with a unique ability to communicate complex concepts in a clear and accessible manner.

Through this book, M. D. Lloyd aspires to guide readers on a transformative journey, helping them orchestrate their own symphony of financial success.

www.ingramcontent.com/pod-product-compliance
Lightning Source LLC
Chambersburg PA
CBHW070927260726
48661CB00003B/866